General Editor:
Patrick McNeill

The Sociology of Schools

3·50

Karen Chapman

THE
SOCIOLOGY
OF
SCHOOLS

Tavistock Publications · London · New York

First published in 1986 by
Tavistock Publications Ltd
11 New Fetter Lane,
London EC4P 4EE

Published in the USA by
Tavistock Publications
in association with Methuen, Inc.
29 West 35th Street,
New York, NY 10001

© 1986 Karen Chapman

Typeset by Hope Services,
Abingdon, Oxfordshire
Printed in Great Britain by
Richard Clay, The Chaucer Press,
Bungay, Suffolk

*British Library Cataloguing in
Publication Data*

Chapman, Karen
The sociology of schools. –
(Society now) – (Social science
paperbacks; 335)
1. Schools – Great Britain –
Sociological aspects
I. Title II. Series
370.19 LC191.8.G7

ISBN 0–422–60210–8

*Library of Congress Cataloging in
Publication Data*

Chapman, Karen
The sociology of schools.
(Society now)
Includes bibliographical
references and index.
1. Educational sociology – Great
Britain – History – 20th century.
2. Sex discrimination in education –
Great Britain – History – 20th
century.
3. Discrimination in education –
Great Britain – History – 20th
century.
I. Title. II. Series.
LC189.C515 1986 370.19 86–1842

ISBN 0–422–60210–8 (pbk.)

Co(B. 38620 (2) /3.50 9 88

Contents

Preface   vi

1 Post-war developments in education in Britain   1
2 Explanations for unequal educational performance   22
3 Gender   61
4 Education and race   81
5 The process of schooling   102

References   129
Index   137

Preface

Everybody experiences education in one form or another, and that is why, I believe, education is one of the most popular topics in sociology. The sociology of education is concerned not just with abstract theory but with the day-to-day experiences of thousands of pupils and teachers.

Education offers a rich and varied field for sociologists. All the sociological perspectives and methodological approaches are amply illustrated by education. Above all, education is accessible for study. Any student of the sociology of education has available ample opportunities to observe the process of schooling and even test out theories. Each chapter in this book ends with a range of activities which can be carried out with a minimum of resources, and will greatly aid comprehension of concepts and ideas.

A problem in writing this book has been that of selection. Since the Second World War, a vast range of research into education has been carried out. Almost weekly, as the book was in its various stages of preparation, new research was being published. Perhaps it is this constant development in the sociology of education which makes it such a fruitful field for the student. I hope I have selected those examples of research which best illustrate the main educational issues.

The central themes are the purpose and effects of education – what it does to the millions of children who enter school at the age of five, how it turns them out at sixteen, or older; who decides what happens in schools. The character of education has changed immeasurably since the War but it remains the major socializing influence of children and determines their future lives. The sociology of education offers an analysis of this socialization process and a major contribution to an explanation of the persistence of social inequality.

For insights into the process of schooling, I should like to thank the students I have taught at St John Rigby Sixth Form College. Some sections of this book started life in hand-outs, and the criticisms of my 'consumers' has been invaluable.

Karen Chapman

1

Post-war developments in education in Britain

Historical background to the 1944 Education Act

The 1944 Education Act is a convenient starting point for a book on the sociology of education because the educational experience of almost all of today's school children results from provisions of that Act.

Between 1880 – the start of compulsory education in Britain – and the Second World War, successive governments had increased expenditure on education; the school leaving age had risen from 10 to 14 and many schools were built, but education was not regarded as a major area for reform or government intervention. However, when Britain entered the Second World War, recruits to the armed forces had to undergo ability testing on a large scale. These tests revealed the inadequacies of Britain's education system, and raised the question of how the country would develop economically after the War was over. The government was forced to consider the quality of the existing education system.

Until 1944, the vast majority of children attended a single school, the elementary school, until the age of fourteen. Here they received 'elementary' or basic instruction in literacy and numeracy, as well as practical skills considered suited to their future role as workers in industry or as domestic servants. Elementary schools were state schools, and were free. Most children who attended them received no more education after the age of fourteen. A minority of children attended private elementary schools. These, along with some children at state elementary schools, transferred at eleven to continue their education at secondary schools. The secondary schools were parallel to the elementary system and were fee-paying. These were called grammar schools. A proportion of places at grammar schools, about one third, were free to those who passed a competitive examination known as the Special Places Exam. This facility did allow some working-class children access to secondary education, but since any child could sit the examination, a large proportion of the places went to children from relatively well-off homes, middle-class children. The schooling system that existed served to divide children on social class lines.

The elementary schools had far worse resources and pupil–teacher ratios than the secondary schools. They were organized under separate, less strict regulations, and there was a wide variation in standards. A minority of schools might provide an education for their children similar to that found in present-day primary schools, encouraging creativity and individual expression. Most schools would not have been out of place in a Charles Dickens novel, with desks lined in military precision, automatic chanting of arithmetic tables, and the learning by heart of long epic poems.

At higher levels of education, opportunities for working-class youth were even more limited. It was estimated that less than 2 per cent of the population had the possibility of going to university. The 1930s was a period of cuts in public expenditure, so the expansion of education at all levels was restricted. In 1926 the Hadow Report had recommended that the school leaving age should be raised to fifteen and that secondary education should be free for all, but the cuts during the following economic depression prevented these recommendations from being implemented.

It was the experience of the Second World War which illustrated more vividly than any government report, the wastage of human resources which resulted from an inadequate education system. Army recruits were found to be extremely unhealthy and many were illiterate. Many more were found who, despite great talents, had been unable to proceed beyond elementary education because their families were in poverty. Michael Young, in his satire on education, *The Rise of the Meritocracy*, commented on the fact that each major reform of Britain's education system had been preceded by wars, and wrote: 'Every child from an elementary school who became an officer in the Hitler war was an argument for educational reform' (Young 1961).

In 1941 the government established the Norwood Committee with the brief: 'to consider suggested changes in the secondary school curriculum and the question of school examinations in relation thereto'. The Committee was also to consider the practical recommendations made by similar committees such as Hadow (1926) and Spens (1938).

An interest in reforming education did not just come from government ministers. During the War the Army created the Bureau for Current Affairs to provide education for the armed forces. It was very successful and demonstrated the potential for educational reform in peacetime. It also had a reputation for encouraging the spread of Socialist ideas. When the Labour Party won their large majority in the 1945 General Election, it was partly attributed to the 'forces vote'; the Labour Party was also during this period a great advocate of educational reform — it is likely that those who had enjoyed some additional educational opportunities, the soldiers, translated that into electoral support for the party most associated with the provision of education for the working class.

The aim of the Norwood Committee was to work out a

structure for education in Britain – a structure which would allow an easy procedure from elementary school to secondary school, thus ensuring maximum opportunity for all.

It is widely assumed that all the evidence presented to the Norwood Committee favoured a selective system whereby passage to secondary school was marked by the taking of an examination, the results of which were to determine the type of secondary school a child would go to. In fact a wide range of educational systems were suggested to the Committee, with many in favour of a single secondary system catering for all abilities. Such schools were known as 'multilateral', now called comprehensive. One such body was the National Union of Teachers, who in 1938 commented on the Spens Report: 'the distinctions made between "academic" and "practical" subjects are largely artificial . . . there should be no attempt to segregate those pupils who will and those who will not, stay at school beyond the age of 16' (from the NUT's comments on the Spens Report, 1938, quoted in NUT 1983). The Labour Party had adopted a policy in favour of multilateral education as early as 1916. The 1945 Labour Government's first Minister of Education, Ellen Wilkinson, was a strong supporter of the idea, but found herself presiding over the establishment of a selective system.

Despite all the arguments against selection submitted to the Norwood Committee, it was, in the end, swayed in the direction of selection to secondary schools on the basis of an academic test at the age of eleven. The educational theory which lay behind this stems from the work of Sir Cyril Burt. This was based on the belief that a child's intelligence was inherited from its parents along with hair and eye colour. Burt – and indeed most educational psychologists of the time – insisted that it was possible to test the intelligence of a child at the age of 11 or 12 with reliability. The results of the test would determine the child's future abilities, so it was logical to provide different types of school to cater for the different levels of ability.

The fact that much of Burt's research has since been found

to be fraudulent perhaps makes it difficult to remember that he was regarded as the authority on child intelligence. (See p. 25). He had been employed by the London County Council, a local education authority, as the first ever child psychologist, and he was extremely influential. It was his evidence to the Norwood Committee that led them to recommend a system based on academic selection at the age of eleven.

Provisions of the 1944 Education Act

The Norwood Committee, completing its deliberations in 1943, concluded:

> 'To the three types of school parity of conditions should be accorded; parity of esteem must be won by the schools themselves. Such a reorganisation offers equivalence of opportunity to all children in the sense in which it has valid meaning, namely, the opportunity to receive the education for which each pupil is best suited for such time and to such a point as is fully profitable to him.'
>
> (quoted in NUT 1983)

In other words, the three types of school proposed in the Report were to be regarded as equal in status.

Compared with pre-War provision, the 1944 Act represented a vast improvement: free secondary education for all, the raising of the school leaving age to fifteen, and, above all, a reversal of the pre-War principle that pupils should be educated according to their social position. This principle had meant that working-class pupils received an education inferior in quantity and quality. The 1944 Act established the principle that children should be educated according to age, ability, and aptitude. In 1938 only 4 per cent of all seventeen year olds were in full-time education. It was hoped that the 1944 reforms would offer undreamed of opportunities to working-class children which would enable them to achieve a higher status. Glass, who examined the British class structure in the 1940s, remarked: 'The 1944 Act will no doubt greatly increase the amount of social mobility in Britain' (Glass 1954).

The 1944 Act did not lay down a specific form of school organization for local authorities to implement. A minority of authorities went straight into a comprehensive system, notably Leicestershire. By 1952 there were thirteen additional comprehensive schools elsewhere in Britain. But the majority of local authorities adopted the idea of academic selection at the age of eleven, and organized their schools into three distinct types: grammar, secondary modern, and technical. This became known as the tripartite system. A child's results in the examination at eleven, the '11-plus', determined which of the three schools he/she would attend. Those who achieved the top marks, regarded as academic, went to grammar schools; the next band, considered to possess technical ability, went to technical grammars, while the rest (who had failed the examination) went to the secondary moderns, which were nearly always new schools.

Why was this system so popular with the local authorities? One reason was the widespread belief in the effectiveness of the existing grammar schools. If they were providing a good education, why alter them? The local authorities believed that the 11-plus examination would allow more children to attend grammar schools. Another factor was the power of the grammar schools. Many of them originated, not in the twentieth century, but many centuries earlier. They were prestigious institutions in their towns and could boast of famous 'old boys'. They possessed organizations of these former pupils dedicated to preserve the traditions of their school.

The politicians who had to implement the Act, even though by now it was a Labour Government, had been educated mainly in the independent or grammar sector, as were the Chief Education Officers who were responsible for local reorganization. What actually happened in each area depended very much on existing provisions and the personal views of the local government officers in charge. Additional grammar schools were rarely provided, and there were very few technical schools. Of those few, nearly all were for boys only.

An important factor in the shaping of education after 1945 was that the system established in most parts of Britain simply confirmed processes which were already in operation. The tripartite system was not, in fact, new. In many areas, the three types of school suggested by the Norwood Committee already existed, often at elementary level. In particular, technical, or vocational, schools existed to serve specific industries. After 1945, few new technical schools were built. They could only be found in large industrial towns. It is not widely known, but there had been attempts to provide secondary education for working-class pupils. Some elementary schools established secondary departments in the late-nineteenth century; however, these did not survive an Act of Parliament designed to tighten up control of education.

After 1945, the aim of most local authorities was to increase the number of children receiving a practical education after the age of eleven, linked to the needs of local industry and commerce. For example, in a town such as St Helens, where the main employers were in glass-making, school pupils would be directed towards that industry, boys into glass production, girls into office and canteen work. It was assumed that only a limited number of children in each area would benefit from a grammar school education, but this was never tested. No local authority made any attempt to assess potential parental demands or even to calculate the effectiveness of local educational resources. This had the effect, later confirmed in research designed to monitor the Act, that a child's chance of obtaining a grammar school place owed as much to geographical location as to 'ability'. In the 11-plus examination, taken in the final year of primary school, the mark needed to enter grammar school was set according to the number of grammar school places available. In effect, the 11-plus examination was to become a rationing device for scarce resources.

While reorganization of the structure was taking place, no

attempt was made to examine what actually went on in schools, to look at the curriculum. Researchers into the system later commented that British schools had an inbuilt tendency to maintain social inequality (Halsey, Floud, and Martin 1956). This neglect of curriculum reform in 1944 was believed to be a major factor in perpetuating the social inequality the Act was supposed to eradicate. The same mistake was to be repeated when comprehensive reorganization took place.

Before the Second World War, children received an education according to their parents' wealth and social class. Generations of children who displayed great abilities in elementary schools were unable to pursue an education after the age of fourteen because of the financial need to earn a living and the cost of attending grammar school. Facilities for adult education did exist but were limited. The 1944 Act was designed to change all this. Its aim was to ensure equality of opportunity to all children, regardless of social class and wealth. Equality of opportunity was supposed to lead to social equality: the possession of a good education in which there were no barriers could break down class distinctions. The working-class pupils who went to grammar schools could enter any profession, leaving their class origins behind.

These aims were worthy but unachievable. Halsey, Floud, and Martin (1956), who examined the record of the tripartite system for several years after it was established, found that the three types of school were just as class-biased as the system they replaced. There had been no significant increase in the numbers of working-class children getting to grammar school. In addition, a child's chances of getting to grammar school were determined by geographical area. (See p. 27). A later study by Jackson and Marsden (1962) examined the fortunes of working-class children at grammar schools. They found that these children were frequently made to feel out of place in the middle-class atmosphere of grammar schools. As a result, many left at the age of fifteen instead of staying on to take O Levels, and a large proportion found themselves in the bottom sets when subjects were organized on that basis (see also p. 27). Floud and Halsey, writing in 1958, commented that a child's academic success

> 'depends as much on the assumptions, values and aims embodied in the school organisation into which he is supposed to assimilate himself, as on those he brings with him from his home.' (Floud and Halsey 1958)

The 1944 Act helped to establish a mechanical means by which all children would, in theory, have access to an equal education, but what happened inside the schools went unchanged.

Comprehensive education

Halsey, Floud, and Anderson summed up the effects of the 1944 Education Act: 'Widespread social amelioration since the Second World War had not removed persistent class inequalities in the distribution of ability and attainment' (1961). By the early 1960s the evidence of the effects of the 1944 Act forced educationalists to think again about the structure of the education system. There was a strong body of opinion in favour of comprehensive schools, where children of all abilities could be educated under one roof. It was also felt socially desirable to mix together children of diverse class backgrounds. Comprehensive schools could, it was believed, end the class bias of selection at eleven and break down class barriers between children. There were also economic factors: maintaining and equipping a single large school in a community was cheaper than keeping separate schools for the different ability groups.

One factor which influenced the way education was to develop in the 1960s was the publication of the Crowther Report in 1959. The Report highlighted the wastage of ability evidenced by the fact that only 12 per cent of pupils continued their education until the age of seventeen; early school leaving was related to social class, not academic performance. The

Report advocated remedies to encourage a far higher percentage to enter sixth forms, including the raising of the school leaving age to sixteen and curriculum changes. The Crowther Report examined the whole range of educational provision for 15–18 year olds and contributed considerable weight to the evidence for working-class underachievement.

A Labour Government was returned in the 1964 General Election, with a definite commitment to the establishment of a comprehensive system. They did not have, however, a clear idea about the nature of these schools. Some believed, like the Prime Minister, Harold Wilson, that comprehensive schools should be 'grammar schools for all', which turned out to be a vote-catching slogan for those with children in secondary modern schools. Others had hopes that the comprehensives would offer a completely new type of education, free of the solely academic grammar school traditions, and dedicated to the establishment of a class-free society.

In 1965 the government issued a memorandum to local education authorities, Circular 10/65, requesting each to submit plans for reorganization of their schools along comprehensive lines. Without the force of law, many LEAs ignored it, or submitted plans designed to be rejected. By 1970, only 10 per cent of LEAs had submitted plans, despite a large increase in educational expenditure aimed at promoting comprehensive reorganization. But from 1970 there was a rapid acceleration in reorganization, despite the election of a Conservative Government who were opposed to Labour's plans. When Labour returned to office in 1974, they enshrined the comprehensive principle in law, with the 1976 Education Act. This was followed by another setback when Margaret Thatcher's administration took office in 1979 and removed from the statute books the compulsion to provide comprehensive schools. This was intended to assist the retention of what were left of the grammar schools. The political chopping and changing which characterized both national and local government in this period had an unsettling affect on education. In Tameside, Greater Manchester, a Labour local authority had reorganized its schools and appointed new head teachers and staff. In the May local elections, the Conservatives overturned the Labour majority and immediately cancelled the reorganization plans. Teachers found themselves allocated to different schools from the ones they had been appointed to, and parents even had to buy a second school uniform for children. When Labour returned to office in the subsequent local elections, the comprehensive plans were restored.

The majority of local authorities now have some form of comprehensive system. Comprehensives are now far more popular with parents than they were in their early days when they had yet to be proved effective. Indeed, when Conservative Solihull attempted to restore a selective system in 1983, vigorous campaigning by a largely middle-class group of parents forced the authority to abandon its plans.

The widespread adoption of comprehensive schooling has not meant the end of selection. Of the 104 LEAs in England and Wales (Scotland operates its education system under separate regulations), 70 still retain a measure of selection. Selection operates in several forms. An obvious one is that former grammar schools tend to be situated in areas of private rather than council housing. This has the effect of ensuring that the majority of pupils at such schools are from middle-class backgrounds. Local authorities have been reluctant to operate a social class quota system for schools. Another form of selection is when a former grammar school establishes a special relationship with primary schools in private housing areas. Allowing first preference for places to children whose siblings and/or parents attended the school is yet another way schools can perpetuate a middle-class bias. Some schools have even failed to establish Special Needs departments on the grounds that it is unnecessary, thus overloading neighbouring schools with pupils with learning difficulties. Parents have been quick to cotton on to such policies. Articulate and

11

knowledgeable parents have achieved a measure of success by appealing to the Secretary of State if their children are allocated a place at a less favoured school.

The 11-plus examination, which allocated children to different schools, has been replaced in the comprehensive system by internal selection. Two thirds of comprehensive schools operate a system of 'streaming'. This means that children are taught in groups according to measured ability in each subject or across all subjects. Some schools divide children just for subjects like mathematics or English, keeping art, physical education, etc. in 'mixed ability' groups. There are wide variations in the age at which children are academically divided. Division may take place in the first, second, or third year of secondary schooling. Some schools allocate children to tutor groups on the basis of the primary school they attended, which may also have the effect of separating children by social class, since primary schools tend to reflect the character of their local community. Whichever method of internal division schools adopt, the whole curriculum is dominated by the examinations at the age of sixteen. Ninety-eight per cent of schools operate an internal selection procedure which leads, at the end of the third year, to separate groups for the different types of examination which exist – GCE, CSE, and, from 1988, GCSE – as well as into non-exam groups.

The independent sector of education

A small proportion of children attend schools which their parents pay for, known as 'independent' because they exist outside state education provision. There are 2,000 of them, ranging from small private day schools catering for primary-age children to 'progressive' schools, established by individuals who wish to practise radical educational ideas, to the old and famous 'public' schools, such as Eton and Harrow, attended by the sons of the aristocracy and wealthiest members of society.

Independent schools are not really independent from the state at all. They depend for their financial existence on a legal anomaly which allows them to register as charities, just like Oxfam or the RSPCA. This gives them tax relief on their income and reduction of rates. The schools also receive allowances to educate the children of members of the armed forces and government employees who work abroad. The taxpayer subsidises the private sector by an estimated £200 – £300 million annually.

Most children at private schools are from wealthy homes. At the 250 most prestigious schools, which belong to an organization called the Headmasters' Conference, 90 per cent of the pupils come from the professional and managerial classes and above (Halsey, Heath, and Ridge 1980).

The products of private education achieve occupational success. Halsey, Heath, and Ridge's 1980 study found that the type of school a person attended was the main factor in occupational success. Particularly in business and managerial occupations, public school boys emerged on top. They were also far more likely to acquire educational qualifications, mainly because private schools are dedicated to intensive examination preparation and have an average of fourteen pupils per class. In all the top positions in society – the legal profession, civil service, armed forces, medical profession, industry, and government – the majority went to independent schools.

Private education appears to be expanding. A big growth occurred when the 1974–79 Labour Government abolished the Direct Grant, the financial assistance which enabled some private grammar schools to provide a proportion of their places free to those who passed an entrance examination. The Conservative Government which replaced Labour in 1979, claiming to assist the low-income parents of bright working-class children, established the Assisted Places Scheme. A central fund was set up from which local authorities could claim, to pay the fees for a few children whose parents' income was below £6,401, to attend local private schools. In

13

fact, very few of the families who have taken advantage of this scheme are from the working class.

Some current developments in education

Education is not a static institution. While there have been no major changes in educational legislation in recent years, changes are taking place which have profound implications for the development of schooling. The two main areas which concern sociologists are the changes being made to the examination system, and the mushrooming of a body outside the control of the Department of Education and Science, the Manpower Services Commission.

The changes to the examination system may be viewed as an issue of who is to control education. By 1988, the GCE and CSE examinations will be amalgamated to form a single exam to be taken by pupils in the fifth year of secondary schooling, the GCSE. This has involved the examination boards, many of them influenced or directly controlled by universities, in a process of negotiation about the nature of the new examinations. The Conservative Government which took office in 1983 favours a tightening of control over examinations and over education as a whole. The 'winners' in the debate about the nature of the assessment of fifth year pupils appear to be those who advocate traditional teaching methods and syllabuses. Teacher-controlled examinations are on the decline and will probably disappear, to be replaced by syllabuses and examinations over which classroom teachers have little control.

An examination of the GCSE proposals shows that they represent a major erosion of teacher autonomy. Control of syllabus content will become increasingly centralized, and education will become even more a tool of the economy than it already is. The new examination boards will have representatives of industry serving on them. The opportunity for teachers to influence syllabuses and methods of assessment will be severely limited. The GCSE examinations – far from helping to increase the proportion of school pupils who gain qualifications, the current trend – look as if they could bring back a return to pre-CSE days, when a minority of fifth year pupils gained qualifications, GCE O Levels.

The question of the new examinations has helped to bring education into the forefront as a concern of the mass media. One issue is the question of 'standards'. Generally, teachers are blamed for the apparently declining educational standards of school leavers. This has occasioned attacks on 'radical, progressive teachers'. A report by Bennett (1976) on primary school teaching methods, which appeared to suggest that traditional methods were the most effective, received far more media attention than is normal for a piece of educational research. One source of criticism of schools and teachers has been industry. In a period of declining job opportunities for school leavers, employers are in a position to be very choosy about whom they will employ. Some have not been slow to use this as an opportunity to attack the educational standards of young people, and, by implication, teachers.

In this atmosphere, the idea of education for vocational preparation has arisen. The body most concerned with this has been, not the education system, but the Manpower Services Commission (MSC). The MSC was established by a Labour Government in the 1970s to enable the growing ranks of unemployed people to retrain in skills in which jobs still existed. Since then, the MSC has far outgrown its original purpose. The MSC runs the Youth Training Scheme (YTS). In the areas of highest unemployment in Britain up to 50 per cent of school leavers may be involved in a YTS programme.

The influence of the MSC is not confined to the provision of training schemes for jobless school leavers. It is becoming a major provider of further education, financing many pro- grammes inside technical and further education colleges, often with separate staff from the mainstream college. Some of these programmes are day-release courses for young people on YTS schemes. In the past, day-release education for young

15

workers was the responsibility of the colleges themselves.

The influence of the MSC is now also being felt in schools, with the establishment of the Technical, Vocational, and Educational Initiative (TVEI) in some local authorities. The TVEI is a programme of vocational education provided for a proportion of pupils, separate from the GCE and CSE courses. The aim of the TVEI is to prepare young people for the world of work while they are still at school. The large sums of money which have been poured into schemes like the TVEI, while mainstream education suffers financial cutbacks, indicate the high value that the current government places on vocational training.

Because of the newness of vocational education, there has not yet been much sociological analysis to contribute to an understanding of its impact on education as a whole. But there are some areas which are already causing concern and have been researched. One area is the issue of equal opportunities. A study commissioned by the Fawcett Society (named after a nineteenth-century feminist) found evidence that girls were not getting the same access as boys to good quality training on YTS schemes (1985). Millman (1984) warns that, without careful monitoring, the TVEI could also perpetuate sex stereotyping (for more on this, see p. 75). She points out the pitfalls of vocational courses designed around the traditional job market. That job market is extremely gender-biased, and, moreover, many jobs which traditionally employed girls are now on the decline.

An important area of concern to teachers and their trade unions is the question of the accountability of the MSC. Councillors who control local education authorities are elected by members of the public at local elections. If the public is dissatisfied with the LEA's record, they can be turned out of office, as frequently happens. LEAs are financed mainly by the rates paid by the public. No-one elects the MSC boards. They receive their money directly from the government. LEAs have a statutory obligation to provide certain levels of education. The MSC provides what it wants, and can withdraw a course or scheme without any notice. This has serious implications in Further Education colleges, where mainstream courses may have been withdrawn to make room for MSC programmes. This situation makes both students and teachers very insecure.

For sociologists it is important that the impact of vocational education should be examined, since it adds a new dimension to what we mean by 'education'. In the book *Unpopular Education*, a critique of government educational policies since the Second World War, the Centre for Contemporary Cultural Studies questions the avowed concern of the MSC that young people should acquire technical skills. (Centre for Contemporary Cultural Studies 1981). The CCCS suggests that the MSC is far more interested in fostering 'good worker attitudes'; its primary concern is to mould and control young people in the interests of the employers. The MSC talks of wanting young people to be 'adaptable'. It could be argued that by this they mean that they want young workers to accept low wages and exploitation. These points are interesting to sociologists because they echo some analyses of the role of education as a whole (see 'functions of education', p. 37).

Understanding education – the role of sociologists

As compared with 1944, children now spend more years at school, many more pass public examinations, the curriculum has broadened, and the school regime is far more gentle and 'child-centred'. The days of Mr Gradgrind, the authoritarian schoolmaster in Dickens's novel *Hard Times*, are gone. Sociologists have constantly been involved in the assessment of the education system as it has developed, and have been actively involved in the shaping of educational policy. It was the research of sociologists like Halsey, Floud, and Martin in the 1950s which led to a reassessment of the provisions of the 1944 Act. A more recent example is the establishment of Educational Priority Areas (EPAs) in the late 1960s. The schools in these areas, generally inner-city areas of social

17

deprivation, received extra money to help improve their quality of education. The EPA policy was in response to evidence presented by research which investigated the relationship between social class and educational performance. The best known example of this research was *The Home and the School* (Douglas 1964). Douglas correlated educational performance with social and material conditions inside working-class homes (see also p. 28). Similar research in America also led to increased expenditure on education in deprived areas in the form of the 'Head Start' programme.

This research has been described as being of the 'political arithmetic' approach. The researchers used empirical methods to take a critical look at an aspect of an unequal society, the education system. The result of this research was a great deal of statistical evidence ('arithmetic') to support the view that the education system contributed to social inequality. Much of the research was funded by governments and bodies such as the Organization for Economic Co-operation and Development (OECD) and its aim was to influence those in positions of power – the politicians. Politicians tend to be influenced only by those findings accompanied by impressive statistics.

The research did not examine what actually went on in schools, but treated them as if they were internally identical, like the 'black box' of an aircraft. Later researchers have felt that it may be more helpful in understanding the process of education to look at attitudes and values in the internal life of schools. This approach developed in the 1960s (although there were earlier precedents, especially in America), and involved attempts to interpret what goes on inside schools. This entails the sociologist immersing him/herself in the chosen aspect of the daily life of schools. Such studies reject the survey method of investigation, such as formal interviews and questionnaires. They use participant observation, tape and video recording, and notebook recording of informal conversations to gain insights into the reality of school life. These studies rarely fall neatly into the categories of the main sociological perspectives, and very often draw no conclusions that can be translated into educational policies, as was frequently the intention of the earlier group of researchers referred to. 'Interpretivist' studies are, however, generally far more entertaining and absorbing to read. One of the first was *Social Relations in a Secondary School* (Hargreaves 1967), which investigates the social effects of streaming, undertaken when the author worked as a teacher in a boys' secondary modern school. 'Classroom Knowledge', (Keddie 1971) demonstrates that children who 'ask questions' in class may be labelled as 'disruptive' if they are working-class, with serious implications for their school careers. *The Education Decision Makers* (Cicourel and Kitsuse 1963) illustrated the role played by guidance systems in American high schools in channelling pupils into school courses at the end of which they had little alternative but to become factory workers. Among the most illuminating recent studies are those which focus on the different educational experience of girls and boys. *Invisible Women: the Schooling Scandal* (Spender 1982) highlights the many and varied ways in which girls are rendered 'invisible' in schools, thus perpetuating male dominance in society.

Sociologists do not now confine their investigations to aspects of life which are easily quantified. All aspects of life in schools are now considered worthy of attention, in order to throw light on the many and varied ways in which children experience education. But although methods of research have changed and become more flexible, the major issue in the sociology of education remains: sociologists are still investigating the factors contributing to unequal educational performance, in terms of gender, race, and social class.

Activities

1 Research the history of your school. Was it originally a grammar or secondary modern, or was it built as a comprehensive? When did it become comprehensive?

What changes have taken place since reorganization? This information will be available from long-serving members of staff or older members of your community. Try to find out what curriculum, discipline procedures, and uniform used to be like.

2 Try to obtain from your local education office the statistics of numbers taking exams at sixteen from, e.g., twenty years ago, ten years ago, and compare them to the present figures.

3 Find out how pupils at your school are allocated to their tutor groups and teaching groups. Is primary school of origin a factor? Are pupils given a test on entry at eleven? Are primary school reports used? Some of this information will be available from teachers.

4 Find a friend or relation aged over fifty-five, and question them about the schooling they received, the age they left, any exams taken, etc.

5 Autobiographies and historical novels often contain vivid descriptions of the schooling of the past. Search through some examples from different periods and compile accounts of different types of education. Examples are: *Hard Times* (Dickens), *Lark Rise to Candleford* (Flora Thompson).

Further reading

National Union of Teachers (1983) Our Children, Our Future. *NUT Education Department. This can be obtained free from NUT headquarters. It contains a brief history of education, and has a useful reading list on the same subject.*

Pedley, R. (1970) The Comprehensive School. *Harmondsworth: Penguin. A classic account of the origins of comprehensives.*

Partridge, J. (1968) Life in a Secondary Modern School. *Harmondsworth: Penguin. This deals with the workings of*

the 11-plus system, streaming, and school organization.
Jackson, B. (1964) *Streaming: an Education System in Miniature. London: Routledge & Kegan Paul. Results of research into the educational effects of streaming in junior schools.*

2

Explanations for unequal educational performance

Intelligence and the IQ debate

Performance in school, whether in essays, tests, or behaviour in the classroom, is frequently regarded as evidence of level of intelligence. A child who receives poor test marks may be labelled as 'slow' or 'unacademic'; one who scores highly may be perceived as 'bright', 'quick', or 'intelligent'. Teachers use these terms to describe their pupils because grading and testing of children is an integral part of school systems.

The 11-plus exam, to determine the type of secondary school a child will attend, has almost disappeared, but many children enter comprehensive schools with a written assessment of their abilities prepared by their primary school teachers, and are allocated to classes in the new school on the basis of these written assessments. The whole of secondary schooling is punctuated by annual exams, culminating in the external exams of GCE and CSE, (from 1988 GCSE) taken by more and more pupils every year. One of the main purposes of schooling would appear to be to test and grade children. The results of testing are claimed to be a measure of ability.

Defining and testing intelligence goes back to the early 1900s. In France in 1905, a doctor, Alfred Binet, devised a series of tests to determine intelligence. These tests were based on the assumption that intelligence would increase with age. Having worked out the average performance for each age group, the performance of an individual child could be compared with that standard. A child who performed below the average for its age group was regarded as retarded, and Binet's tests were used to exclude such children from schooling. The fact that those labelled as retarded were often from very poor homes was not considered worthy of investigation. Similar tests were also adopted with enthusiasm by the armed forces, and used to allocate First World War recruits to regiments and ranks.

Underlying Binet's theory was the view that intelligence was inherited by children from their parents, that it was part of the genetic structure of a person. The whole of a child's future potential was a result of that inheritance.

One of the most influential British advocates of intelligence testing was Sir Cyril Burt. He believed that 80 per cent of a person's intelligence was attributable to heredity, 20 per cent to the person's home environment. As schools psychologist for the London County Council before the Second World War, Burt administered tests to hundreds of children, and also worked with twins who had been separately reared. He claimed that the measured ability of such twins was so closely correlated that heredity must be the key factor in determining intelligence since the twins had quite clearly experienced different environments. It was the persuasiveness of Burt's statistics which led to the selective system which resulted from the 1944 Education Act.

IQ (intelligence quotient) tests have been used widely in the British and American education systems. Believed to be 'objective', that is, without bias, they have been employed to allocate generations of school children to different types of secondary schools and ability groups within schools. Eysenck, a former pupil of Burt, who has produced evidence for the inheritance of intelligence, has argued that the exact amount of intelligence which is inherited is not important – it is sufficient that it exists.

Small-scale investigations have produced evidence that it is the environment rather than genes which most influences intellectual developments. Skeels (1966) studied a group of children in an overcrowded orphanage, considered too retarded to be adopted. He moved them to a smaller, more home-like environment and arranged individual care for each one as well as a variety of toys and stimulating material. Two years later Skeels found that the average IQ for the group had risen to 92.8, an increase of 28.5 since they left the orphanage. The control group who had remained in the orphanage had reduced their IQ score by 26.2 points, down to an average IQ of 60.5. Moreover, the experimental group retained their improved IQ scores. There have also been studies of mentally handicapped adults who showed improvements in IQ when moved to more stimulating environments.

The research of Burt and of Skeels is concerned with how children acquire intelligence. An underlying assumption of these arguments is that the measuring of intelligence is socially necessary. But before intelligence can be measured, it must be defined. It has been, in fact, notoriously difficult to obtain an acceptable definition of intelligence. It could be said that an IQ score is a measure only of something called IQ, not of intelligence as a whole. Bowles and Gintis (1972) point out that while there is an undoubted relationship between high occupational status and high IQ, this could just as easily be explained by social background as by inherited intelligence. They argue that, in the USA, IQ serves to legitimize the class system and the social institutions which help to reproduce social classes; by attributing the possession of wealth to high IQ, structural reasons for inequalities of wealth are concealed.

It could be argued that exact knowledge about the origins of intelligence has no important social implications. The

24

genetic theory does not rule out the possibility that IQ could be improved by enriched environments. Even if definite proof that intelligence was inherited was available, the very existence of even some environmental influence makes it probable that the level of attainment in schools could be raised by improving the schools. It is this view which has motivated most educational developments since the 1944 Act.

In the USA, Jensen (1969) has applied the genetic theory to race. He claimed that black Americans scored an average of 15 points less than whites in IQ tests, and that this was attributable to genetic differences. Critics of Jensen, disturbed by the implications of his statements, argue that the black experience in the USA has historically been one of extreme poverty, sub-standard education, and discrimination by whites. Given all these social factors, a comparison of black and white performance in IQ tests is simply not valid. The unequal performance reflects the cultural and racial bias of the tests, rather than the inferior intelligence of black people. Through the use of IQ tests, a far higher proportion of black children than white children have been labelled as 'mentally retarded' and sent to special schools. Some black parents have even taken school boards (local authorities) to court to protest that their children have been made the victims of biased tests. (There will be a full discussion of race and education in Chapter 4.)

More recently, genetic theories suffered a setback when detective work by a medical journalist, Dr Oliver Gillie, discovered that Sir Cyril Burt had produced fraudulent statistics to support his claims. Gillie failed to find any documentary evidence for the existence of Burt's two named research associates who had apparently administered tests to twins. In the USA, a psychologist, Leo Kamin, examined Burt's statistics. He points out that the correlations of intelligence between twins were far closer than is normal for correlations in scientific experiments. In five pieces of research published between 1948 and 1966, Burt finds correlations between the IQ scores of identical twins reared separately a constant 0.771. Kamin comments: 'The kinds of data collected by scientists in the real world simply do not behave with such incredible stability' (Eysenck *versus* Kamin 1981). Kamin also draws our attention to other flaws in Burt's work: it is extremely difficult to find identical twins who have been reared apart. No-one, apart from Burt, has ever attempted such a study. Burt also compared the intelligence of close relations. Again, his is the only study. Normal scientific research gives a detailed account of procedures employed in obtaining results and references to other work. Burt does none of this. Nor does he even state which IQ test was used in his work. In his research into adults, he does not even claim to have administered tests, relying instead on personal interviews. Kamin concludes: 'There is no doubt whatever that in any discussion of IQ heritability, the entire body of Burt's work can be discarded . . . the remaining data cannot even establish that the heritability of IQ is significantly greater than zero' (Eysenck *versus* Kamin 1981).

Burt's supporters have found it hard to defend his work against the damaging evidence. Much of their own work has been based on Burt's data. Jensen has excused Burt by reference to 'carelessness' in his methods; Eysenck uses the word 'forgetful'. Burt's official biographer, originally an admirer, attributes the fraud to 'an ailing and elderly man.'

Social class and educational achievement

Intelligence tests formed the basis of 11-plus selection. Since these tests were believed to be unbiased, the idea was that bright children from working-class homes would not be handicapped by their environment and could be enabled to attend grammar schools, thus increasing the pre-War percentage. But very soon, doubts were being raised about the effectiveness of 11-plus selection. In the early 1950s, Hertfordshire Education Authority examined its use of intelligence testing and found a close relationship between success in the tests and social class. It was found that the percentage of children from working-class homes admitted to grammar schools had fallen between 1952 and 1954. This stimulated much sociological research throughout the 1950s and early 1960s aimed at documenting unequal educational performance and determining its cause.

The first wave of this research is typified by *Social Class and Educational Opportunity* (Halsey, Floud, and Martin 1956). Their findings demonstrated that the 11-plus system of selection had not significantly increased the number of working-class children going to grammar schools; those that did were far more likely to leave at the minimum age of fifteen than were middle-class children. They suggested the following reasons:

1 The uneven provision of grammar school places, far fewer in areas with a larger percentage of working-class in the population.
2 Financial hardship of working-class parents, being unable to afford the uniforms and 'extras' expected in grammar schools.
3 The clash of cultures which may arise when a child from a working-class home enters the middle-class environment of the school.

In conclusion, the authors listed two main factors governing educational achievement:

1 Home encouragement and attitudes of parents.
2 Material factors at home and school.

The conflict between working-class and middle-class ways of life was further explored in *Education and the Working Class* (Jackson and Marsden 1962), a study of eighty-eight working-class pupils in a Yorkshire town who gained grammar school places. Despite parental encouragement in academic work, many of these pupils were obstructed in their achievement by the material circumstances of their homes compared to the majority group of middle-class children: such material conditions included noise levels in the home and crowded housing conditions which made private study difficult. These pupils also experienced street conflict with their former peer group, who attended secondary modern schools. Jackson and Marsden's sample children, when they became adults, tended to regard themselves as classless and generally moved away from their neighbourhood. In employment terms, they had done better than their working-class peers, but not as well as their middle-class schoolmates. The study suggested that the admission of a few working-class children to grammar schools at the age of eleven had done nothing to reduce class divisions.

The most influential research into social factors on educational performance was *The Home and the School* (Douglas 1964). Douglas's main concern was the wastage of talent caused by the inequalities of the educational system. He found that there were insufficient grammar school places to meet demand. An analysis of the class backgrounds of grammar school pupils revealed that the majority were middle-class; most grammar school places and the best schools were in areas of private and not council housing. Douglas listed a range of social factors which influenced school achievement:

1 The social class of the parents.
2 The level of parental interest and encouragement. If this was high, average test scores were three points higher.
3 Size of family and position of child in the family: elder children did better, the younger members of a large family did worse.
4 Deficient care of babies in large families.
5 Conditions in schools: the larger the class, the lower the test scores. Good primary teaching could compensate for material deficiencies in the home and lack of parental interest.
6 Streaming reinforces the process of social selection: middle-class children are found in the higher streams.

Douglas concluded: 'The evidence set out in this book gives strong reasons for believing that much potential ability is

28

wasted during the primary school years and misdirected at the point of secondary school entry' (Douglas 1964).

Douglas proposed an improvement in primary school teaching and an increase in nursery schools to give working-class children the stimulus lacking in their homes. This picture of the culturally deprived working-class home was given further weight by the publication of several reports into child development, notably the Newsom Report, 'Half our Future' (1963) and the Plowden Report into primary schools (1967). These were to result in some changes in the direction of educational policy in Britain. Similar research findings in America also resulted in a corresponding shift in educational policy, which will be dealt with further on in this chapter (see p. 33).

The three studies described above all focus on the material conditions of the working-class home and/or parental interest to explain working-class educational failure. Two measures of parental interest were the number of times parents visited their child's school, and what teachers said about parents, which is hardly a valid source of information. If working-class parents do pay fewer visits to schools, could it be, for example, because working-class jobs generally have longer hours than middle-class ones, rather than a lack of interest? Alternatively, could it be that working-class parents do not feel welcome in the middle-class atmosphere of schools, something which would not bother middle-class parents? Midwinter, who developed the EPA project (see pp. 34, 37) in inner-city Liverpool, found no evidence that working-class parents lacked an interest in their children's education. When the schools encouraged their presence, they were only too pleased to visit.

The idea of cultural capital

Bourdieu (1973) proposes an alternative view of the relationship between working-class culture and educational attainment. He states that parents transmit to their children cultural capital as well as material conditions. Cultural capital is a system of deeply internalized values which determine attitudes towards educational institutions. These values determine behaviour in school and the level of educational attainment. Schools play a role in the perpetuation of inequality by penalizing those who do not conform to middle-class standards of behaviour, while setting criteria of achievement which favour children with middle-class 'cultural capital'. Teachers are themselves the products of the education system whose aim it is to transmit the culture of the ruling class: 'The education system reproduces all the more perfectly the structure of the distribution of capital among classes' (Bourdieu 1973).

Bourdieu is not suggesting that one culture is superior to another, but that the power of one class, the ruling class, enables it to impose its culture on others. The effect in schools is that ruling-class culture is the only legitimate one and defines what constitutes 'knowledge' and 'intelligence'. Children in schools are assessed according to how well they have absorbed the dominant culture. If they possess cultural capital which corresponds to the demands of the school, they will be rated as 'intelligent'. Bourdieu does not describe exactly what constitutes this culture, nor does he explain how it finds its way into the school curriculum. He implies that cultural capital is more important than wealth in explaining educational success, but does not discuss the relationship between these two factors.

English studies of educational success have shown that family culture as well as material conditions are influential in educational attainment, and that the type of school also plays its part (Halsey, Heath, and Ridge 1980). Culture might well affect selection processes within the education system, but it is family income which influences length of time spent in education, attitude towards public examinations, and likelihood of a pupil applying for higher education, all of which also affect subsequent occupational choice and success.

Language and class

In the late 1950s Bernstein started his work on exploring the relationship between social class and communication. His theory of language is based on the belief that each social class generates a system of communication shared by members of that class and specific to it. Bernstein called these systems 'codes'. These codes consist of meanings, symbols, and relationships expressed through language. The codes can be ranked: from the restricted code at one end of the continuum to the elaborated code at the other. People who use the restricted code (generally from the working class) assume meanings in their language; their language is dependent on the context in which it is spoken – it is particularistic. The elaborated code, more found in middle-class speech, is context independent, it is universalistic. Bernstein illustrates the codes as follows:

> Elaborated code:
> 'Three boys are playing football and one boy kicks the ball and it goes through the window the ball breaks the window and the boys are looking at it and a man comes out and shouts at them because they've broken the window so they run away and then the lady looks out of her window and she tells the boys off.'

> Restricted code:
> 'They're playing football and he kicks it and it goes through there it breaks the window and they're looking at it and he comes out and shouts at them because they've broken it so they run away and then she looks out and she tells them off.'   (Bernstein 1973a)

The extracts are from a study of the language of five year olds. They are describing a series of pictures and have been asked to tell the story. The first extract is spoken by a middle-class child. The listener does not depend on seeing the picture to understand the story; the child's language is 'context independent'. The second extract, spoken by a working-class child, depends on seeing the picture to understand the story – the language is 'context dependent'.

Bernstein argues that working-class children do less well in schools than middle-class children because:

'the school is necessarily concerned with the transmission and development of universalistic orders of meaning . . . educational transmissions . . . are based on performance rules which the middle class child embryonically possesses. Class regulates the elaborated codes of education and the family.'   (Bernstein 1973b)

Bernstein's theory has some serious implications for education:

1 Working-class language is inappropriate in schools. If working-class children want to do well, they must adopt a linguistic code which devalues the family experience from which they come.
2 The language of everyday is distinctly different from the language of learning.
3 Pupil performance has less to do with the education they receive in schools and more to do with what they bring to school.

Bernstein has been criticized for offering inadequate empirical evidence to support his theory. He uses an imprecise definition of social class and does not demonstrate the link between thought-processes and language. He has, however, been very influential, since he appears to provide a more concrete insight into the relationship between class and educational performance.

In the USA Labov examined the language of black children in ghetto areas of New York, a group which, like English working-class children, had low levels of educational attainment. Labov was particularly concerned with the idea that lower-class (the term used in America) speech was in some way inferior to 'standard English'; there seemed to be a suggestion that lower-class people were incapable of abstract thought. Bereiter and Engelmann (1966), whose research with black children came to similar conclusions to Bernstein's, had reported that the children 'communicated by gestures, single words and a series of badly connected words or phrases'. They even appeared to doubt whether black children possessed a language as such at all.

Labov criticized the racial prejudice inherent in Bereiter and Engelmann's work, suggesting that too many teachers of black children hear not merely children speaking a different dialect, but the 'primitive mentality of a savage mind' (1969); Bereiter and Engelmann were accurately describing the behaviour of black children in school with a (usually) white teacher. Labov illustrates the way that the context in which language is spoken can influence styles of speech: hundreds of black children in New York schools were given a series of interviews. In a typical one, a boy is interviewed by a white person. The child is withdrawn and monosyllabic. In the second interview, the interviewer is black and the boy is more fluent and relaxed. Finally, the black interviewer invites the boy to bring along a friend and offers them crisps. This time the boy is articulate and confident – completely different from how he appeared in the first interview. Labov argues that the children's language reflects the social factors at play in the situation. With the white interviewer, the relationship represents one of white domination over black. With the black interviewer, the relationship is less threatening for the child.

Labov gives other illustrations to demonstrate that the language of American blacks is rich in abstract concepts and that the child is 'bathed in verbal stimulation from morning to night'. This demonstrates that there is no connection between the speech characteristics of street culture and success in the classroom.

Cultural deprivation – its translation into policy

Evidence which pointed to the cultural deprivation of working-class children has been responded to in educational policies. The publication of research described earlier in this chapter, such as Douglas (1964), and the Plowden Report (1967), resulted in the adoption of the idea of 'Educational Priority Areas' or EPAs. Some parts of England and Wales, particularly in the inner-cities, were designated as priority areas for the receipt of extra funding and resources. To overcome the problem of high turnover of staff in these schools, teachers would be offered a supplement to their incomes to work in them. The intention of the EPA policy was outlined by Halsey (1972) as follows:

'(a) to raise the educational performance of children.
(b) to improve the morale of teachers.
(c) to increase the involvement of parents in their children's education.
(d) to increase the 'sense of responsibility' for their communities of the people living in them.'

(Halsey 1972)

An area acquired its EPA status by virtue of its measurable indexes of poverty: its housing conditions and the proportion of its children receiving free school dinners. Educational factors included the average reading ages of the pupils and school attendance and truancy rates.

There were similar policy moves in the USA. The Coleman Report (1966) investigated the lack of educational resources available to black and other minority groups. This Report did not find glaring differences between facilities in black and white schools, and concluded that the poorer performance of black children was a result of their family background. The Coleman Report pointed to areas of the education system where improvements could be made. This involved discriminating positively in favour of schools with a high proportion of black pupils, to reduce the tendency, noted in the Report, for schools to reinforce the inferior position of disadvantaged children.

What the Coleman Report did was to distinguish between the idea of equality of opportunity, a preoccupation of earlier studies, and equality of results. This demanded the active involvement of schools in enabling disadvantaged groups to improve their levels of attainment. It was not enough simply to ensure that each child had a school to attend: schools must also increase the proportion of those who achieved academic success. The rationale behind this was that social inequality could thus be radically reduced.

As part of a general anti-poverty programme, the American government initiated the 'Head Start Project'. As in England and Wales, the project aimed to compensate for deprivation in the homes of poorer children, particularly in black ghetto areas. The 'head start' provided was in the form of pre-school education and the provision of breakfasts in some schools, so that the children could start the day with proper nourishment. The British and American schemes have come to be called 'compensatory education'.

Assessments of cultural deprivation theory and compensatory policies

Cultural deprivation theory has been criticized because it implies that working-class children are culturally deficient; the adoption of government programmes has institutionalized the concept of deficiency, which has led to the labelling of such children in schools. Keddie (1971) rejects the idea that working-class and black children are in any way culturally inadequate – they are simply different. To attribute educational failure to cultural deprivation implies that it is the children's own fault, like blaming poverty on its victims. Attention is also drawn away from the basic structural causes of educational inequality.

The policies of compensatory education which have arisen from cultural deprivation theory have likewise come in for some criticism. Jencks (1972) asserts that the programmes of reform were never effective in reducing inequality. Education is not the main avenue through which social inequality is perpetuated. Using the same data as the Coleman Report,

Jencks argues that educational reform is no substitute for more fundamental change – schools are marginal in the process of social stratification. He rejects Coleman's findings that show a high correlation between education and later occupation, arguing that it is the economy of society which is the key determinant of social status. Jencks's assertions can be taken in two ways: from a revolutionary point of view, that a fundamental change in society is needed, or, from a conservative point of view, that money spent on improving education is money wasted.

Thornbury (1978) refers to the 'EPA myth'. The EPA policy was, he asserts, simply one more incidence of 'papering over the cracks in the walls of the urban classroom'. The criteria for establishing an EPA were drawn up by individual local authorities, which led to striking inconsistencies. The financing of the schemes was also uneven. An LEA with more faith in the EPA concept might inject additional cash into its schemes.

In agreement with Jencks (1972), Thornbury characterizes compensatory policies as a diversion from the root causes of educational inequality – he illustrates this with reference to a study of the views of primary school head teachers in London EPAs. All those interviewed were convinced that educational solutions could solve the social problems of their pupils. Halsey, the veteran educational researcher, takes a different view. In the first EPA Project Report (1972) he describes the success of community involvement in the designated schools, and noticeable improvements in the quality of teaching in them.

Other supporters of the schemes claim that results have been undramatic only because EPA projects were insufficiently funded. Only 150 schools were given EPA status, not the 10 per cent or 3,000 recommended by the Plowden Report. Therefore what was actually achieved could only be a drop in the ocean of educational inequality. The additional resources given to schools in disadvantaged areas were warmly welcomed by teachers, and excited the envy of the suburbs. The projects also led to new school buildings being erected. A significant benefit was the expansion of pre-school, or nursery, education, one of the main recommendations of the Plowden Report. Midwinter (1972), in a description of the Liverpool EPA project, insists that it was never claimed that the EPA policy was the answer to the problems of multiple social deprivation. He argues that the development of community education must be part of a general programme of community regeneration. However, the key role schools play in the community makes them the lynchpin of developmental programmes. Even if the EPA schemes in Britain or Head Start programmes in the USA never led to the dramatic improvements in working-class educational performance that were optimistically envisaged, they did show the 'evident potential for revolutionary reforms in education' (Bowles and Gintis 1976).

The functions of education

The theories of educational inequality so far outlined concentrate on the level of working-class attainment in school. But the education system does not exist in a vacuum; it is only one part of a total society composed of many institutions. What are the functions of education in that society?

There are two major perspectives on this: the Functionalist perspective and the Conflict perspective. Functionalism is closely related to the theory of society as a meritocracy (see p. 41). Conflict theory may be further divided into Marxist and non-Marxist varieties. Both perspectives and their subdivisions offer an analysis of the position of education in society as a whole and the role it performs for that society.

The Functionalist perspective

The Functionalist analysis of the education system relates schooling to the needs of the economy. It argues that inequality is a natural feature of society, since people are born with unequal talents. The functions of the education system are to allocate and recruit people to the range of positions in society. For society to function, there has to be a method of ensuring that all the necessary occupational roles are filled: far more factory workers are needed than doctors, for example.

The foundations of the functionalist theory were laid by Durkheim, a French sociologist who was writing when state education was in its infancy. He saw the development of education as being directly related to changing needs and ideas in society. He demonstrated, in a history of education in France, that all great social movements have resulted in changes in education. One example of this was the Renaissance, which marked the end of the Middle Ages in Europe, a 'rebirth' of culture, science, and learning, financed by the growth of European trade and production. The Renaissance led to the creation of educational institutions, particularly universities, to develop knowledge and contribute to the wealth of society.

Durkheim believed that the function of social institutions was to promote and maintain social cohesion and unity. Education performed this role by 'the methodical socialisation of the young generation' (1956). By this he meant that education developed those values and intellectual skills needed by children to perform the role in society to which they had been allocated. This ensured the survival and development of society.

The Functionalist analysis of society is based on the idea of consensus, in direct opposition to the Marxist view of conflict. Consensus means that people agree on the basic values of the society in which they live, and recognize its benefits. It is in everybody's interests that consensus exists, and therefore anything which threatens stability must be kept under control. The family, law, and the educational system are agencies of this control. They ensure that society operates smoothly. The discipline structure and organization of children in schools are part of this process.

Schooling helps children to develop and discover their talents so that, when they join the workforce, they will enter an occupation suitable for them and needed by society.

It is an assumption of Functionalism that all pupils have equal opportunities. If children leave school with unequal levels of attainment, it is a result of individual differences of intelligence and endeavour. These are measured by grading, testing, and the examination system, which help to allocate children to their appropriate occupational roles. Success in examinations is determined in such a way as to ensure that only a minority achieve it, since only a minority of jobs require high levels of skill. The minority who achieve success in school examinations have further educational opportunities made available after the minimum school leaving age. This provides society with the right levels of skill needed for it to advance.

Unequal wealth and status in society are also seen as the result of unequal intelligence. Doctors earn more than refuse collectors since society values great skill, and the training for a medical career is long. The education system is at the service of all; anyone with talent, who is prepared to work hard, can climb the ladder leading to wealth and status. All children have equal opportunities to climb that ladder. Factors such as class, race, and gender have no effect on success.

The historical context of Functionalism The Functionalist view of education dominated educational sociology in the USA in the period after the Second World War. While British sociologists were concerned with education as a vehicle for the achievement of social equality, in America the preoccupation was with improving America's economic and military position in the world. An improvement in the education system was seen as the ideal way to achieve this. In the historical period known as the 'Cold War' (a description of the hostile relations between America and the Soviet Union at that time), the American government wanted to produce scientists and engineers in the quantities needed to prevent the

Soviet Union from gaining technical superiority. This goal acquired even greater urgency for the American government when the Soviet Union was first to put a satellite into space.

Functionalism fitted in with this approach to education, because of its concentration on the economic and technical needs of society. It almost reached the stature of an official ideology, with its leading exponent, Talcott Parsons, broadcasting for the American government on 'Voice of America', a propaganda radio station relayed to Communist countries. Clark, in a Functionalist analysis of education, was quite explicit about a political role American education could play in turning back 'the expanding thrust of totalitarianism abroad' (1962).

Criticisms of Functionalism In the light of more recent educational research, the functionalist approach has come under fire on several points:

1 The assumption that there is a correspondence between the technical needs of the economy and the subjects taught in schools is false. Most of the school curriculum has no direct vocational significance.
2 The educational level of the workforce in modern capitalist societies is actually in excess of that needed to keep up with the technical requirements of industry. Braverman (1974) argues that, increasingly, most jobs are being de-skilled under the impact of technology.
3 There is no correlation between the educational level of workers and their efficiency and productivity for their employers.

Schools do play a role, as Functionalism suggests, in allocating pupils to positions in the workforce, but the process is not neutral. It is not based solely on merit, but strongly influenced by class, gender, and race. It could be argued that, far from schools promoting attainment, they actually reduce the aspirations of some pupils, such as those from the working class, ethnic minority groups, and girls. In

40

support of this, Cicourel and Kitsuse (1963) present evidence that it is the social class of pupils that determines the course of study to which they are assigned in American high schools. Working-class pupils are persuaded to take non-academic courses which severely limit their career opportunities when they leave school.

Finally, the Functionalist idea of a consensus of values is oblivious to the fact that modern industrial societies are multi-cultural, composed of people from a wide range of origins and cultures. There are very few shared values, if any. If there is a dominant culture, it has been imposed on a culturally diverse society. Education is one of the means by which this dominant culture is transmitted, and there is evidence to show that this culture discriminates against pupils on the basis of class, race, and gender.

The meritocracy thesis

Closely related to the Functionalist perspective is the idea of society as a meritocracy. This theory is based on an assumption that a person's wealth and position in society are allocated according to individual merit. Inequality is explained by differences in intelligence and talents. The education system in a meritocratic society offers equal opportunities to all children to discover their talents and place them in appropriate occupational roles. The psychologist Herrnstein (1973), an advocate of the inheritance of intelligence, gives an example of the theory in practice. He argues that because only a small percentage of people are intelligent enough to do highly skilled work, society honours this intelligence by paying them more. Parsons, the leading exponent of Functionalism, also favours the idea of meritocracy, arguing that modern industrial society is based on achievement and not inherited wealth.

The educational reformers of the period after the Second World War viewed education as a means to achieve a more egalitarian society. To some of them, egalitarianism meant a meritocracy. They aimed to create an education system which offered the best possible opportunities to all children, in contrast to the pre-War period when the education children received was determined by their parents' wealth.

Meritocracy is based on the view that intelligence is unequally distributed, and that social inequality is an inevitable outcome of this. Implicit in this is a belief that education cannot alter a child's intelligence, but can only bring out what is naturally there. Critics of the meritocracy thesis point to the overwhelming evidence that educational achievement results from family background and social class, not from individual merit. Bowles and Gintis (1976), writing of the USA, argue that the education system disguises the inherent social inequalities of society by spreading myths about meritocracy. They demonstrate that while educational statistics always show a high correlation between occupation and qualifications, it can be shown that people of a high social class are far more likely to obtain qualifications than members of the working class and ethnic minorities. Educational improvements since the Second World War have not significantly altered this fact. This is as true for Britain as it is for the USA.

A meritocracy would not actually get rid of social inequalities. It would simply operate as a more efficient mechanism for allocating people to occupational positions in society. This could be said to be the main intention of most educational policy changes since the War. A classic criticism of meritocracy is Young's novel *The Rise of the Meritocracy* (1961), a satirical comment on post-War educational policies, set in the future. It suggests that the ability of individuals to move between social classes would be increasingly curtailed in a society in which talent was the only determinant of social position. The end result would be a society in which stratification was more rigid than that which had originally existed.

Halsey, who has been investigating educational inequalities over a long period of time, rejects the idea that post-War educational reforms brought Britain closer to a meritocratic society (1980). He suggests that, while the quality and quantity of education available to the poor has undergone a massive improvement, so has education for the well-off. As with other aspects of welfare provision in Britain, such as the National Health Service, it has been the middle class which has most taken advantage of free secondary education. Their children had the advantage in the selective system established by the 1944 Act, and continue to benefit from comprehensive education. This has also been the case in a whole range of other countries with similar education systems to that of Britain. To reconcile the indisputable fact of educational inequality with a belief in meritocracy inevitably leads to a view that social class determines intelligence. Such a view can be discounted by the evidence of many research projects which have repeatedly demonstrated that even when working-class and middle-class children have the same IQ, middle-class children do better in the education system and obtain jobs with higher status and pay.

Conflict theory

Conflict theory has two branches: (Marxist and Weberian). It differs from Functionalism in its rejection of consensus and 'value-free' sociology. What it has in common with Functionalism is the way in which it regards education as serving an economic purpose for society.

Marxist conflict theory The Marxist theory argues that all societies are formed out of class struggle. Capitalist society, of which Britain and the USA are examples, was formed out of the struggle between the landed aristocracy and an emerging class whose wealth was based on industrial production and trade. Karl Marx (1818–83), the originator of Marxism, called this emerging class the bourgeoisie.

Marxism views the means of production – industry, land, finance, and commerce – as the basis of society. Every other institution originates from the means of production and exists

43

to maintain them. Your social class is determined by your relationship to the means of production. If you are an owner of means of production – a landowner, industrialist, or banker – you are part of the ruling class, or bourgeoisie. If you own nothing but your labour power, you are a member of the working class, or proletariat.

These two classes – the former very small but possessing great power, the latter the majority of the population but possessing relatively little power – are locked into constant conflict for control of the means of production. For example, a pay strike represents an attempt by the organised working class to wrest a greater share of the wealth they have helped to create. A basic premiss of Marxist theory is that at a particular stage in the history of capitalism, the working class will win power and society will be transformed. It will be a Socialist society, where no individual will be able to own means of production. There will be common ownership of all wealth-creating institutions. Social classes and inequalities of wealth and opportunity will disappear since their social basis will no longer exist.

In a capitalist society all social institutions exist to serve the interests of the ruling class and maintain it in its position of power: the family produces and sustains the next generation of workers; the legal system controls those who challenge the laws of private property; education teaches the children of the working class their proper place in society and provides them with the knowledge and values required to create wealth for the ruling class when they become workers.

Bowles (1978), an advocate of Marxist conflict theory, traces the development of the education system to demonstrate that schools were provided by the state, not to give children equal opportunities, but to meet the need of capitalist employers for a disciplined and skilled workforce. In addition, he argues, schools are a mechanism for social control to help maintain political stability. Inequalities in the education system help to reproduce the class system from one generation to the next. Whatever goes on in individual schools, they

44

cannot escape their inevitable function, which is the reproduction and legitimation of the class structure.

Conflict theorists view the education system as an agent in the reproduction of the class structure. Bowles and Gintis (1976) show how the system of rewards and sanctions in operation in American high schools reinforces behaviour and attitudes favourable to capitalist society. Bowles and Gintis have also applied conflict theory to the controversial area of IQ (1972). They argue that IQ is not a significant determinant of economic and occupational success as claimed by its advocates. The key determinant is the individual's position in the class structure, a position that schooling has helped to create.

Althusser (1969) argues that education is a part of the 'ideological state apparatus' of capitalism, along with the armed forces, police, and legal system. Education functions through the means of ideology, the ideology of capitalism. The education system is in a unique position in that it can command an obligatory and free audience of all children. What school teaches children is the ideology of capitalism. This includes rules of 'good' behaviour, respect for the existing social order (the status quo), and a belief in the 'fairness' of the system. To back up ideology, schools also employ methods of repression, such as punishment, banishment, and selection.

As the division of wealth becomes increasingly unequal, capitalism faces growing problems of social control. Schooling plays a role in this, with its emphasis on discipline and respect for authority. Schools use a variety of methods to control pupils: through the curriculum, through the way in which children are organized in schools, and through the hierarchical staffing structure, which mirrors the hierarchy of the wider society.

In order for society to be capable of change, each different form of society contains inherent weaknesses which contribute to its eventual overthrow. Ideological control of oppressed peoples is not total. It is impossible to conceal the contradic-

45

tions of an economic system which creates great wealth but keeps large numbers of the population in poverty, homelessness, or unemployment. People are not simply passive receivers of capitalist values which so clearly provide them with little benefit (unless they are members of the ruling class). The capitalist system is under constant challenge through the activity of trade unions, working-class political parties, and other forms of protest. Education also contains elements of challenge to the system, which is one reason why the establishment of education by the state lagged so far behind the development of the capitalist system itself. It was feared that educating the working class would open their eyes to the true nature of the society they lived in. Encouraging children to think and discover things for themselves raises the possibility that they will use that knowledge to change society rather than support it.

Weberian conflict theory Weberian conflict theory is derived from the work of Max Weber (1864–1920). Weber's work shares common ideas with Marxism (for example, Weber regarded social class as an important determinant of an individual's position in society). However, Weber questioned the basic Marxist assumption that the character of all social institutions were derived from the nature of the economy. In his work, Weber could be said to have 'engaged in a posthumous dialogue with Marx' (Cuff and Payne 1979). He aimed specifically to refine the Marxist concepts of power and class, and argued that social change was a result of many factors, not just class conflict.

An important Weberian concept is that of 'status groups'. Status groups are groups of individuals who have in common their status, the amount of prestige that society accords them. Status can be derived from economic wealth, power, or social class, but there are also groups in society who possess high status without wealth or power. Such groups earn their status, perhaps, from the occupation they follow.

Collins (1971) applies the idea of status to education. He

argues that the main role of education is 'to teach particular status cultures, both in and outside the classroom'. Conflicting interests, rather than economic forces, have changed the education system. Collins refers to Weber's analysis of traditional education systems such as that of dynastic China to illustrate the dominant role of cultural interests in schools. In ancient China, the scholars had a higher status than the wealthy merchants. The merchants placed a high value on education in order to secure for their children the status accorded to scholars.

Collins characterizes the rapid growth of educational certification as barriers which those in power place in the way of certain groups. These barriers help to maintain the superior position of the powerful status groups. Collins's thesis is not supported by empirical research carried out in schools. He refers instead to a study of the requirements of employers when recruiting staff. These employers emphasized normative values rather than technical skills. Their educational requirements were designed to attract employees who had internalized the goals of the firm. Attitudes were more important than skills.

Although Weber rejected Marx's economic determinism, many of his ideas concerning the role of social institutions draw similar conclusions. Like Marx, Weber argues that the machinery of the state – laws, police, courts – enables the ruling group to keep in power. The ruling group maintains its legitimacy in the eyes of the population by control of ideology. In this, the education system plays a key role. It is on this aspect of the role of education that modern advocates of Weberian conflict theory place most emphasis.

The historical context of the Marxist perspective   Marx's analysis of capitalist society was written in the mid-nineteenth century. Marx never wrote specifically about education. The education system was seen as a part of the superstructure of society; control of knowledge and ideas lay with the ruling class. In the *Communist Manifesto* (1848) Marx wrote that 'the ruling ideas of each age have ever been the ideas of its ruling class'. Education systems (there was no state education at the time Marx was writing) were the means by which the ruling class maintained their control over ideology. Marx argued that significant social change cannot be achieved by changing the education system because that system is organically related to the needs of the economy.

In very few countries have Marxist principles been applied to the education system, the longest lasting being that of the Soviet Union. (See p. 49). In the capitalist world, since the late 1960s, sociology experienced a growing interest in Marxist ideas. The adoption of a Marxist perspective to throw light on the functions of education did not result from an uncritical support of the Soviet system. Indeed, many Marxist sociologists would assert that the Soviet Union is not a true Socialist society, and educational and other inequalities are evidence of this.

Karabel and Halsey (1979) suggest that educational sociology was influenced by Marxism because of the failure of Functionalism to offer an adequate explanation for educational failure. Moreover, government educational policies had been based on a Functionalist analysis and these had failed to achieve equality. There is also a social context for the popularity of Marxist ideas. The 1960s saw the end of the post-War economic boom and the growth of unemployment. This provided the backcloth for much political and social conflict. There was a sharpening of class, racial, and national tensions. 'Change and upheaval expressed the spirit of the 1960s' (Karabel and Halsey 1979). The political instability of the period was expressed in a rise in militancy among university students. In the USA much of this took the form of resistance to compulsory military service, since America was engaged in the unpopular Vietnam war. In France there was a direct relationship between student and trade union struggles, resulting in a near-revolution in May 1968, known as the 'May Events'. Britain was also the scene for much student political activity: on international issues such as the Vietnam

48

war and South African apartheid, against the authoritarian manner in which universities were administered, and to fight rent rises in halls of residence. As in France, many students allied themselves to working-class industrial struggles. Even school pupils were affected, and an attempt was made to form a school section of the National Union of Students.

Gouldner (1971) characterizes these social movements as a symptom of the failure of Functionalism, particularly in the field of education. The student and class struggles exposed the myth of a society based on consensus. The atmosphere of political criticism in universities, where sociological theories tend to get developed, is conceivably a factor in the rejection of consensus sociology which occurred in the 1960s.

Criticisms of the Marxist perspective   There are two angles from which to criticize the Marxist perspective. The first is to examine its application in the Soviet Union, where a proletarian revolution in 1917 established a society based on the state ownership of the means of production. In the early days, after the 1917 revolution, Soviet education policy meant ensuring that all had access to basic education. Under the former regime education had not been free, and a large percentage of the population, adult and child, were illiterate. In the 1920s, Soviet educational theory was recommending techniques similar to the 'progressive' methods currently practised in British primary schools. From the 1930s this trend was reversed. The concerns of Soviet educationalists of that period sound very similar to some of the issues raised in education in the West today: poor discipline, falling standards, young people unfit for work, and delinquency. Progressivism was replaced by a traditional framework, with complete authority given to head teachers.

It is interesting to compare the outcomes of the Soviet education system with those of Britain and the USA. Although Communism is supposed to remove all class distinctions from society, the patterns of achievement and failure in the Soviet Union have similarities with our own. A survey of school

49

leavers (1966), quoted in Lane (1978), reported that students whose parents had a peasant or working-class background were far more likely to leave school at the earliest opportunity than those of middle-class origin. Access to higher education seems to be similarly class-biased, although the available data is not very up-to-date. It has been estimated that only between 10 and 20 per cent of all university students are of peasant or worker origins. Even at polytechnics, higher education institutions for the study of industrial skills, middle-class students predominate. A study of Soviet education appears to confirm the Functionalist view that education prepares young people for their role in society. Soviet education helps to transmit the culture of society, although this is done in a far more explicit way than in Britain and the USA. Soviet industry has depended on the education system for a supply of trained technicians. With the abolition of inherited wealth, education is a more influential determinant of a person's occupation than in capitalist societies, but as Lane says, 'the cultural forces generated by family and parental occupation have asserted themselves' (1978). Thus an examination of the effects of Soviet education could be said to throw doubts on the Marxist assertion that a society without class divisions leads to educational equality.

The second angle from which to criticize Marxism is that of rejecting it as 'economic determinism' – analysis of *all* social phenomena in terms of their relationship to economic forces. Wrong (1980) suggests that both Marxism and Functionalism offer an 'oversocialised' view of human beings, almost entirely shaped by society, with no independent will of their own. Bowles and Gintis, advocates of the Marxist view in the USA, have been criticized for their faith in a Socialist solution to the problems of society. As described above, the Soviet education system experiences problems very similar to those of the capitalist world. Many people automatically associate Socialism with the Soviet Union, and this serves to divert attention from a serious consideration of the educational theory of Bowles and Gintis.

Marxists are often criticized for lack of empirical evidence in their studies. Althusser (1972) applied classic Marxist theory to education without any reference to empirical evidence. Bowles and Gintis use official statistics to support their views, a source of data which is not impartial.

There is much less criticism of Marxism in the field of sociology than there has been of Functionalism. This is possibly because Marxism is more flexible than Functionalism, since it accounts for social change. Most of the criticisms which have been raised could in fact equally be applied to Functionalism. Critics of Marxism who refer to the experience of the Soviet Union are undermined by the assertion of many 'neo-Marxists' that some of the preconditions of Socialism are absent in the Soviet Union and other East European countries. In the field of philosophy, however, writers have questioned the underlying assumptions of Marxist theory and its political conclusions. It is necessary to accept these assumptions and conclusions in order to accept the applications of Marxism to education.

The Interactionist approach

Conflict and Functionalist theories of education are 'Positivist'. This means that they see social behaviour as governed by cause and effect in the same way as the behaviour of organisms in natural science. In research terms, this implies that human behaviour can be objectively measured. Positivist theories often use a biological analogy to illustrate the workings of society: society is like a living body which is dependent on the smooth functioning of its parts. Just as the body contains mechanisms designed to keep all the parts in working order, society tries to ensure that its parts – social institutions and human individuals – are functioning properly. Social instability or change occur when a part of society is in conflict with the whole.

Interactionists criticize Positivism for its characterization of humanity as entirely shaped by social forces. Positivism attributes no importance to meanings, intentions, and the active participation of individuals in the construction of social reality. Interactionism is not a perspective in the same way that Functionalism or Marxism may be called perspectives. Those who support the approach do not share basic premises and concepts. Nor does Interactionist research employ a predictable methodology. The approach originated early in this century, but it remained a minority tradition until the 1970s. Interactionism derives its title from its insistence that it is social interaction which shapes reality, and not any external social system. People are not passive. In any social interaction, individuals are like actors, playing out a role which they have decided is appropriate to the situation. Schools offer a rich source of illustration of this. A child may be a 'model' pupil in a classroom where the teacher respects him/her and allows him/her to express himself/herself. The same child may act in a disruptive way in another classroom where he/she perceives the situation as threatening. Labov's description of the language of the black child, (see p. 33) also illustrates this.

The Interactionist approach seems tailor-made for studies of education because of its refusal to be tied down to a limiting methodology. Research influenced by Interactionism focuses on the internal workings of the education system. The meanings constructed by the participants of education – teachers and especially pupils – are as valid an area of study as examination results. Phenomena which Positivists explain by reference to the social structure are examined from a different standpoint. In an examination of working-class educational 'failure', for example, Keddie (1971) examines the meaning of 'class' for teachers (see also p. 105). Willis (1976), who combines a Marxist orientation with an Interactionist approach, demonstrates the relationship between working-class pupil culture and pupil failure (see p. 107).

Interactionists also turn their attention to the way organizational aspects of schools shape social reality. Hargreaves (1967) and Lacey (1970) examined the streaming systems in their schools, which divided pupils according to academic performance.

Ineractionist studies illuminate very effectively, and often entertainingly, processes within the education system. Some may be criticized, however, for going to the opposite extreme from Positivism. Few Interactionist studies have anything to say about the structural origins of intentions, meanings, and role-playing. They demonstrate that working-class children fare badly at school because of the way in which they interact with teachers, but they do not explain how social class comes to have a significance in society, or where it comes from. Willis (1976) is one of the few exceptions to this tendency.

Sarup (1978) argues that Interactionism neglects a consideration of structural conflict in society. It has no understanding of historical change and ignores the material conditions of existence. It implies that people should seek change through the way they think, without questioning how thought is constructed. Sarup is not entirely negative about the Interactionist contribution to our understanding of education. He asserts that it offers a valuable analysis of the nature of knowledge, and of the relationship between social stratification and knowledge. This aspect of education will be dealt with in Chapter 5, p. 120.

Education and social mobility

A major concern of the perspectives on education is the relationship between education and social class. The conflict perspective, in particular, asserts that the social class origin of a child is a far more important determinant of its future than the education it receives.

Some sociologists have looked at changes in groupings within the class structure and attempted to relate them to education. These changes constitute what is called social mobility – movement from one social class to another. It can be measured by investigating changes in occupation from one generation to the next, usually from father to son. Measurement of occupations involves ranking them according to their status in society, based on the five groupings of the Registrar

General. These are Social Classes I to V, and are used in the ten-yearly censuses (classification) of the British population.

Social mobility between generations has been used to demonstrate the flexibility of capitalist society. It has also been used to demonstrate the success of post-War educational expansion. The classic study of mobility was carried out by Glass in 1949. This showed that most mobility was short-range, between occupations in the same class band, and that very few people crossed the manual/non-manual barrier; there were virtually no new entrants into the highest positions in society, and, likewise, unskilled manual workers showed very little movement.

Glass's study was conducted with a sample educated before the 1944 Education Act. The most recent large-scale study of mobility was carried out in the 1970s. This used a sample of 10,000 adult males, and was intended to discover whether or not social policy changes since the War had aided the process of social mobility. Women were excluded from the study on the grounds that they would primarily be involved in domestic labour and were economically dependent on their husbands from whom they derived their class position. In their study of the impact of education, Halsey, Heath, and Ridge (1980) found that 32 per cent of the working-class sample had remained at school beyond the age of sixteen; in the 1930s the proportion was 9 per cent. There had also been an increase in the percentage of working-class pupils staying at school until the age of eighteen, but less dramatic than the previous figure; the percentage of working-class people going to university had increased fourfold since the 1930s. But it was clear that it was the middle-class sample who had most benefited from education. Classified in the study as the 'service class', of these members of professional and managerial occupational groups 79 per cent stayed at school after the age of sixteen, with similarly large percentages staying until eighteen and going to university.

This research appears to indicate a high degree of occupational mobility. Only one third of the sample remained in the same social class as their fathers. Thirty-one per cent had moved up, 18 per cent down, the rest remaining in the same grouping. This could be explained by the expansion in the availability of professional and managerial jobs and a decline in that of semi-skilled and manual jobs. The more the groups in the study are sub-divided, the more mobility there appears to be. If, however, the lowest three groups are added together, the picture is different, showing rather aptly how statistics can be applied to almost any argument. Heath (1981) suggests that the amount of mobility measured depends on how people are classified. In a study of recruitment to élite occupations, he demonstrates that access to the 'top' is extremely limited. He concludes that inequality persisted, not because the poor did not aspire to success in educational and occupational spheres but because the privileged conspired to keep them out. It has to be said that the system of education brought in by the 1944 Act has intensified the relationship between social class and achievement, not reduced it.

Because studies of inter-generational mobility involve examining people who have left school and are established in a job, the studies which have taken place use samples who have been educated mainly under a selective system. By the 1970s, when Halsey, Heath, and Ridge's study commenced, only half of all school children over the age of eleven attended comprehensive schools. It will be a few more years before it is possible to study mobility between two generations wholly educated in a comprehensive system. Studies of comprehensive education until now have concentrated on the internal workings of schools. It has been demonstrated that the selection processes which so characterized the tripartite system still exist in the comprehensive system. Organizational procedures such as streaming can produce the same social and educational effects as if the pupils have attended separate schools.

Can schools make a difference?

The research and theoretical perspectives outlined in this

chapter give a pessimistic impression of the ability of education to alter the fundamental inequalities which exist in our society. It appears that changes in education have done no more than dent the class structure. For a contrasting viewpoint on the effects of education there is currently only one modern piece of research. This is the study entitled *15,000 Hours* carried out by a team of child psycologists (Rutter *et al.* 1979). Their intention was to investigate the implications of previous research that education had no effect on children's futures.

15,000 Hours (the total number of hours of compulsory schooling) is a study of different aspects of the educational experience of 2,000 pupils at twelve comprehensive schools, all in the same working-class borough of London. The authors found that there were significant differences in the behaviour and attainment of pupils in the different schools. The evidence for this was derived from observation of children and discussions with teachers. School statistics such as attendance records and examination results were also examined. The differences between schools could not be explained solely by the proportions of low-ability or badly behaved children at the schools. All the evidence pointed to differences in the schools themselves as being the main factor for differential performance and behaviour. The behavioural and academic records of pupils in each individual school were also remarkably stable. Finally, there was a relationship between pupils' behaviour and examination successes. Factors such as size of school, condition of buildings, and administrative style of the school appeared to have had no influence at all.

The evidence of *15,000 Hours* appears to contradict the findings of all the major educational research which has taken place since the Second World War. In attempting to explain the consistency of results in the schools studied, the authors refer to the values and attitudes which prevail, characterizing the atmosphere in the individual schools – the behaviour of pupils was shaped and influenced by these values. This ensured the perpetuation of a particular standard of behaviour and academic results.

The research has been criticized for a variety of reasons. The basic criticism has been of its methodology. The authors argue that social factors external to schools have little impact on pupil performance, but their definitions and measurements of these factors are unclear. They include factors which are actually a product of schooling received before a pupil has entered secondary school – such as primary school records, hardly 'external to school'. Important factors affecting pupils are left out, such as gender and ethnic group. A. Hargreaves (1980) suggests that this led to a serious underestimation of the influence of social background on pupil performance at school, hence an over-emphasis on the effects of individual schools. The authors use terms like 'good behaviour' and 'good schools', but are unclear about what they mean. When talking about the values prevalent in the particular schools (the ethos), they refer to items such as the emphasis on homework, and how frequently pupils use the school library. These might be valid measures of values, but they are also partial, representing value judgments by the authors about what is important in schools, and many other factors are omitted.

The novel conclusions of *15,000 Hours* earned it a great deal of media attention, but they do not stand up to examination. The study itself only refers to one other piece of research which backs up a small part of its findings. No other study since its publication has found similar evidence about the effects of schools. Pessimistic though this may seem, the overwhelming evidence presented by the sociology of education is that social inequality continues to reassert itself in each new generation of school pupils. Education is not a major force for social change.

Activities

IQ testing

1 This is best administered by a teacher as a group activity. Obtain one or more examples of IQ tests. *Know Your Own IQ* by H. J. Eysenck, Penguin Books, contains some. Complete one or more tests. Score them. Note down how you felt doing them. Did you find them easier than a normal school test? Compare your score(s) with your average performance in school exams or set work. Discuss your views on the validity of IQ tests.

Language

2 Choose an extract of difficult academic writing. (Sociology books are a good place to search!) 'Translate' the extract into everyday language. Consider whether your translation makes the passage any easier to understand, or whether it in fact changes the meaning. Note down which ideas and concepts are best expressed in 'jargon'. A variation on this is to write your next essay for sociology in everyday language and make the same notes. Discuss in a group why technical language is sometimes necessary.

Social class

3 School/college records of former pupils are sometimes available on the shelves of the library. In these are names, father's occupation, and first job of the pupil after leaving school, as well as details of qualifications gained. Obtain records for a particular year, choose a manageable list of pupils (e.g. one tutor group), and divide the pupils into categories according to father's occupation, using the Registrar General's Scale. See if there is any similarity between the qualifications and first job on each pupil and their social class group. It would be useful to do this with the records of several years to determine whether there are any noticeable changes in the relationship over time.

EPA policies

4 NB: This exercise is only applicable if you are close to an EPA area or Social Priority school. You will be able to find out this information from your District Education Office. (If you are actually a student in an SP school, your task will be much easier.)

Get permission to visit an EPA primary school or an SP secondary school. Interview teachers who have worked at the school prior to its designation about changes in the school as a result of the policy. Some questions to ask might be: What additional resources came to the school after designation? Did the extra payment to teachers help to reduce the turnover of staff? How did the curriculum change?

Perspectives

5 The perspectives make an ideal subject for a debate. Individual students can take the role of defender of two opposing perspectives. Taking the opposite role to your own beliefs (playing the 'devil's advocate') is a useful way of understanding the perspectives.

Further reading

Bowles, S. and Gintis, H. (1976) Schooling in Capitalist America. *New York: Basic Books. Not easy to read but a useful account of the Marxist/conflict theory perspectives. Chapter 6 outlines the close relationship between the development of education and the needs of capitalist industry.*

Douglas, J. W. B. (1964) The Home and the School. *London: Panther. This is the classic account of the effects of social class on educational performance. It has been reprinted many times. Important because of the educational policies it inspired. Useful for its detail and an account of its methodology.*

Heath, A. (1981) Social Mobility. *London: Fontana. Contains lots of useful data showing the relationship between education and social class, including data used in the Oxford Social Mobility Studies by Halsey and others.*

Jackson, B. and Marsden, D. (1962) Education and the Working Class. *Harmondsworth: Penguin. Easy to read and full of detail.*

Lane, D. (1978) Politics and Society in the USSR. *London: Weidenfeld & Nicolson. Massive, covering the whole range of USSR society. A good and detailed section on education, for those interested in this area.*

Sarup, M. (1978) Marxism and Education. *London: Routledge & Kegan Paul. A readable discussion of current educational issues and a useful outline of Marxism.*

3

Gender

The social construction of gender differences

A recent growth area in educational research has been the issue of gender. When educational inequalities were first examined, the effects of being a male or female pupil were not considered relevant to educational performance, even though women have protested about unequal access to education for over 300 years. The universal secondary education provided by the 1944 Act was intended as a solution to class inequality. Inequality between male and female was simply not considered an issue – reflecting the expected roles of men and women of the time. On the surface, the provision of free secondary education for all boys and girls appeared to offer equal opportunities to both. The fact that far fewer girls than boys went on to further and higher education was not regarded as problematic.

It took a growing awareness of gender inequalities in areas outside the field of education, such as in pay and the world of work, to stimulate interest in the effects of gender on schooling. The Equal Opportunities Commission was established to monitor and enforce the Equal Pay Act (1970) and Sex Discrimination Act (1975). Attention was focused on social inequality between men and women, and in particular on the origins of gender inequality.

This has inspired a decade of sociological research into the effects of early socialization and the education system – mainly by researchers committed to the principles of equal opportunities. Much of this research not only demonstrates that inequalities exist, but reveals the processes in schools which discriminate against pupils on the basis of gender. The research in this field is increasingly policy-oriented – that is, it seeks to influence the educational policy makers in order to achieve real equality in the education system, proposing specific measures to counteract the effects of gender conditioning.

Early socialization as it relates to education

An examination of gender and education must start with the question: What have children learned before they commence school? Observe any group of infant school children and it is possible to spot distinct differences in the way girls and boys play and learn.

The biological argument

In the past it was widely assumed that these differences were a result of genes, and were therefore pre-determined. Psychological studies of very young babies appeared to show differences between male and female in many aspects of neonatal (newborn) behaviour. If sex differences emerged so early in life, it seemed as if they must be biological rather than social in origin. It was believed that these babies were far too young to have felt the influence of society upon their behaviour. Such biological reasoning is generally to be found in the research of child psychologists, who have been criticized by sociologists for ignoring the effects of the social environment on child development. For example, Piaget, who remains influential in the field of child development, argued (1932) that human behaviour is an external display of internal, biological tendencies. Since most teachers will have studied the ideas of psychologists like Piaget during their training, it is very likely that they regard differences between the behaviour of girls and boys as entirely natural.

Social conditioning

Sociologists explain sex differences in behaviour by demonstrating the powerful influence of social conditioning on young children. Ann Oakley, in *Sex Gender and Society* (1975), presents in detail the evidence that, from birth, babies are treated differently according to sex, by the people who care for them. There does not appear to be any evidence that genetic sex differences exist other than those relating to the reproductive organs of male and female. There is no doubt, however, that socialization patterns for male and female are differentiated from birth and it is therefore important to examine their impact on educational behaviour.

Reinforcement

Young children learn their social roles from the behaviour of members of their family and the expectations placed upon them. Much of early childhood learning takes place through imitation and reinforcement: imitation of behaviour they observe within the family and reinforcement of correct behaviour by the family. For example, a girl may meet disapproval if she fights with another child; she will also observe in her home a distinct division of labour in domestic tasks based on gender. There will also be differences in the type of work her parents do outside the home. Television programmes and advertising also help to maintain this

63

gender-differentiated picture. In each aspect of child upbringing distinct messages may be observed relating to gender roles. Children learn what being a boy or girl means from the day they are born. When they enter school, which can range from under five, in Britain, to six or seven in different parts of the USA and Europe, they will already have had several years of gender learning.

Children spend most of their pre-school years engaged in play. Much of what children perceive as the real world is derived from play. But children do not freely choose what they play with. Those choices are made by parents and relatives and will reflect the assumptions adults make about male and female play. A stereotyped imagery of playthings is also maintained through advertising, particularly on television.

Children also acquire skills from play. The acquisition of motor skills has been well documented by psychologists studying child development. But while a child is acquiring skills, he/she is also absorbing attitudes and values. Dolls and tea-sets are not neutral agents in the process of socialization. They are a crucial part of the message that the expected role for females is to be involved in domestic activities. Likewise, the construction sets and active play typical to boys are informing them that they will be expected, in adult life, to play an active part in the world of work. Research shows that children as young as three years of age will make distinct gender-biased choices when presented with a range of toys (Oakley 1975).

Role modelling

Members of a child's family act as gender-role models, not just in the clothes they wear, but in the domestic division of labour in the household. In the majority of homes it is still female members who do most of the housework and child care. When young children have been questioned about the work they themselves do in the home, it has been shown that parents assign differential domestic tasks to boys and girls.

Girls' tasks will tend to be more kitchen-based, and they will usually be expected to do more housework than their brothers; boys, if asked to help out at all, will be assigned to the garden or garage. *Spare Rib*, the feminist magazine, featured the views of younger readers protesting about the way in which their brothers were not expected to participate in domestic tasks (*Spare Rib* November 1981, no. 112).

Even though only a minority of households with dependent children now conform to the traditional image of housewife-mother/bread-winning father, children's pictures of their parents invariably portray this stereotype. Men earn one third more than women and do distinctly different types of jobs. These factors will inevitably influence a child's perceptions of the world of work, involving notions of which jobs have higher status, which jobs are 'harder', and which have a higher salary.

Early school experience

Children start school with well-developed ideas of what constitutes 'correct' male and female behaviour. The conditioning that they received before they started school will underlie much of their behaviour at school, both at 'work' and in play.

Differences in ability

It has been demonstrated through research that girls and boys, at different stages of their school career, possess different abilities. Nicholson (1984) shows that boys appear to perform better than girls in tests of spatial ability. One example of such a test requires a child to find identical shapes on a page. Another shows jigsaw pieces from a whole picture and asks the child to indicate where on the picture the pieces belong. But there are areas of performance where girls do better than boys. In tests of verbal ability girls appear to perform better than boys.

65

Girls seem to be better readers than boys – and a higher proportion of backward readers in schools are boys. The Assessment of Performance Unit, a government-funded organization involved in educational testing, has found distinct gender differences in mathematical ability (1980) and language (1981).

Biologists have speculated that the Y chromosome which males possess contains a 'visuo-spatial' gene, but even large-scale tests comparing the abilities of parents and their male and female children have failed to establish the importance of such a gene, (Gray 1981). Social explanations appear to be more persuasive. The Newsom Report (1963) found that girls were spoken to more than boys, leading to girls having a better verbal ability at school; boys were given toys which served to develop their spatial and motor skills (for example, construction sets), which encouraged them to show greater interest in related subjects at school. There has been a great deal of testing of children for gender-related differences in educational performance, but ultimately the results are inconclusive. While some differences have been found, these are often too small to be of much significance and could equally validly have been the result of chance. Despite this, however, there is evidence that both teachers and pupils themselves perceive differences, and this shapes the expectations of teachers and the self-concept of pupils.

The primary school curriculum

Gender stereotyping can be found in all aspects of the primary school curriculum. The basic skills of literacy and numeracy are taught using materials which reflect the reality of the outside world. Reading schemes often show the most extreme examples of bias, the best known being the Ladybird *Key Words* series. The series has been updated over the years, most obviously in the clothes worn. These books follow the daily lives of Peter and Jane, who appear to have a housewife mother, frequently depicted in a kitchen, and a breadwinning father, rarely shown, depicted with a car or mending something. The updating has not acknowledged any changes in the traditional roles of men and women. In book 3a, Peter speaks 30 times, Jane only 15. In the illustrations, Peter is clearly shown as the more active of the two; Jane is generally on the sidelines of any action (1974 edition, currently available.) The cumulative effect is of a girl who is passive and satisfied by domestic activities, while boys are shown as physically active and dominant.

Bias is less obvious in mathematics, yet Whyte (1983) points out that females are notably absent in junior mathematics textbooks, and mathematical problems are geared to boys' interests, with the result that quite young children regard it as a male subject.

The rest of the primary school curriculum displays similar gender bias: history books concentrating on male exploits, geography topics about men working (for example, deep-sea fishing or mining). Clarricoates (1980) shows that teachers frequently choose project topics specifically to interest boys, to avoid their possible disruption of the class. Teachers assume that girls will accept any topic.

The same assumptions are made about general reading books, both by teachers and publishers. Boys are 'known' to be reluctant readers, so a careful choice is made of books containing characters and plots with whom they can identify. Girls are 'known' to read almost anything. In the primary school it would appear that females are 'invisible' (Spender 1982), as far as the curriculum is concerned. When they do appear, it is frequently in a stereotyped and distorted manner: research into female portrayal in children's books revealed that out of 58 books examined, of the 25 female characters pictured (including some depicted as furry animals), 21 were shown wearing an apron (McRobbie and McCabe 1981). With such imagery pervading the early school experience, it is easy to see that children are receiving the message that men and women are destined to inhabit different social worlds.

67

The organization of children in primary schools

Divergence of the sexes is encouraged in schools, not only by curricula, but also by the way children are organized. Whyte (1983) illustrates this with the following examples: many schools, built in the late-nineteenth and early twentieth centuries, still retain separate 'girls' and 'boys' entrances; the sexes are still lined up separately when queueing for activities. They are listed separately in registers; they are seated separately, and where a uniform exists, boys and girls wear different clothes, with girls discouraged or banned from wearing trousers. Differences between male and female are also emphasized in the manner in which teachers address children, reprimanding girls for noisy behaviour, asking boys to lift heavy objects.

Free play in primary school

Play is an important part of early education. Usually children are allowed free choice in this, and can select their favourite objects and equipment. Whyte (1983) refers to the 'familiarity syndrome' which directs children to choose toys which they have at home. In fact, free play is not at all 'free'. Free choice can actually restrict the access of one sex to certain types of toys. For example, boys may monopolize Lego in a manner which prevents girls from even trying to use it. Girls may also discourage boys from approaching the Wendy House. A study of infant play in Wigan (1984) highlighted the different use boys and girls make of the same equipment, whereby the Wendy House became a fort when boys were using it.

Teacher expectations

It would be unreasonable to expect that teachers do not share the stereotyped assumptions that the general public make about the sexes. The view that girls are better behaved than boys, while boys are more aggressive than girls, leads to differential treatment of children. Whyte (1983) asserts that the misbehaviour of girls gets less of a reaction than that of boys. This carries a message about who gets the attention. These assumptions would appear to lead to a self-fulfilling prophesy: pupils tend to live up to the expectations placed upon them, so that boys indeed end up 'naughtier' while girls appear to be more quiet. One writer has suggested that boys are at a disadvantage in the predominantly female atmosphere of the primary school (Sexton 1970). Girls are more frequently rewarded and therefore perform better, whereas boys are in conflict with the rules and standards expected by teachers, and hence do less well academically.

It seems that girls in primary school do perform better than boys, but this position is reversed by the end of compulsory education at sixteen. It appears that the conditioning of girls to learn passively works to their disadvantage in the more competitive secondary school, which can be seen most clearly in the option choices and external examination entries of boys and girls. Whyte remarks:

'In the school life of one child there may be a thousand such apparently trivial and unrecorded interactions. The child learns, as if s/he had been taught, that certain games, activities and even physical spaces are for girls or boys. That perception is reinforced by some of the common rules and practices of the school.' (Whyte 1983)

Secondary schooling and gender

On leaving the primary school, the majority of children today attend a mixed-sex, comprehensive school. It has been established that, across the curriculum as a whole, there are no significant gender differences in measured ability. IQ scores for male and female are indistinguishable. Girls do appear to perform better in verbal tests, while boys achieve higher scores in tests of visual–spatial ability, but there is no

69

convincing evidence that general ability is affected by biological sex.

As outlined in the previous section, research into gender and early schooling has shown that girls and boys are conditioned by the social institutions in which they live to adopt the attitudes and aspirations considered appropriate to their gender. This has nothing to do with actual ability, but by the end of compulsory schooling at the age of sixteen, girls and boys will be sitting for distinctly different patterns of external examinations and will achieve different results; they will express different occupational aspirations and, if able to find a job, there will be divergence in their employment. Some will go on to higher education, but here, also, can be found distinct gender differences in courses followed.

The attitudes of teachers and peer groups

'Teachers find it hard *not* to be affected by the assumptions of the world in which we live' (Deem 1978). Assumptions about the abilities and attributes of male and female have been shown to lead to discriminatory treatment of pupils. One manifestation of this is the way in which teachers address pupils. Within a class, pupils themselves have reported that boys are referred to by their names, while girls are referred to as 'the girls'. 'Three strong lads' are frequently asked to help move heavy objects, while girls may be asked to serve tea to visitors. An article about sexism in science in the magazine *New Scientist* (20 May, 1982) described a science lesson in which the teacher (male) challenged the boys to drink from a beaker which was being used to demonstrate the principles of filtration, and teased the girls for their timidity. Dale Spender (1982) video recorded mathematics lessons in a school with a strong commitment to equality. Boys were far more likely than girls to be asked to solve a problem and were given far more attention; even the seating arrangements reflected divisions, with girls occupying the marginal positions outside the direct gaze of the teacher. Spender (1980) has also drawn attention to the use of language, arguing that, through language, women receive the powerful message that they are marginal in society. Most terms of insult are applied to women, not men. In a *New Society* article (8 September, 1983), secondary school girls expressed their feelings about the injustice of a language which seems to emphasize their inferiority and the advantage that gave to boys.

The Sex Discrimination Act and measures to reduce sexism

Since 1975 it has been illegal to discriminate against a person on the grounds of sex. In the field of education, Section 22 states that it is unlawful for an educational establishment to discriminate against a woman by refusing her access to a school, by restricting her access to any facilities or services, or by 'subjecting her to any detriment'. In practice this means that all school subjects and activities shall be available to all pupils. Girls may not be excluded from metalwork, nor may chess clubs refer only to boys. In the vast majority of mixed schools, the craft subjects, traditionally the most gender-biased area of the curriculum, are taught in rotation so that all pupils can sample them for a short time. The clause in quotes, above, is supposed to ensure that the informal procedures of schools do not undermine the principles of sex equality. An example of this is the highlighting of the disadvantages for a girl if she chooses a non-traditional option, such as being the only girl in the class, or reminding her of potential teasing from the boys. Teacher attitudes which lead to jokes about a boy's ineptitude on the sewing machine or the cry-baby who cuts her finger in woodwork would also, under the terms of the Act, be considered discriminatory. It is, however, notoriously difficult to prove sex discrimination. It is asking a great deal of a young teenager to challenge the banter or subtle bullying of a teacher. The pressure from the peer group to conform to gender-typed behaviour also ensures that few pupils will question the assumptions made about them by teachers in school.

Those committed to achieving genuine sex equality have pointed to the need for a positive commitment on the part of the whole school to eradicate discriminatory practices. This entails examining every aspect of school life, not just option schemes. Some local education authorities have adopted specific policies along these lines and some schools have appointed a member of staff to implement equal opportunities. There are also organizations which have been formed to tackle the problems of specific areas of the curriculum: Girls and Mathematics Association (GAMMA), Girls into Science and Technology (GIST), and Women in Science and Engineering (WISE) exist to encourage more girls to enter these non-traditional fields by providing schools with information, speakers, and mounting campaigns. Such efforts are considered necessary as it is believed that the effectiveness of legislation is being undermined by the social context in which people operate.

The curriculum

The Sex Discrimination Act has not radically altered the pattern of option choice which may be observed in schools. Table 1 shows a typical array of examination entries.

Previous sections have described the informal processes which serve to channel pupils into gender-defined subjects. Whylde (1983) shows that a bias towards males exists throughout the curriculum of secondary schools. She brings together a collection of articles dealing with the attitudes to women inherent in every school subject. History, for example, is his story, preoccupied with the actions of men; when women do appear, it is usually in a domestic role, despite the evidence that in all periods of history, women have played a variety of active roles. The typical school history syllabus in fact distorts reality. In art, it would appear that there are few women artists worthy of mention, an assumption challenged by Judy Chicago (1982) in her account of the problems faced by female art students.

Table 1   GCE entries, by sex 1973–74

GCE O levels	no. of entries female	male
English literature	34,888	22,833
geography	25,733	34,314
social science	485	188
religious studies	12,299	7,315
music	3,284	1,484
classical studies	1,178	727
French	32,054	19,070
German	7,377	3,978
computer studies	7,153	15,636
physics	18,889	47,396
chemistry	27,647	3,555
electronics	36	387
biology	36,809	22,788
psychology	3,930	870
geology	1,100	2,688
woodwork	45	3,515
metalwork	16	2,492
home economics – food	21,339	1,686
home economics – clothing	2,156	4
all other subjects	232,986	259,472
total entries	469,404	450,398

Source: Joint Matriculation Board, Annual Report 1983–84.
Note: this is not a complete list of all subjects taken, just those showing significant gender differences.

Frith (1981) discusses the typical diet of novels read as part of English syllabuses. Teachers welcomed the more realistic novels which came onto the syllabuses in the 1960s, particularly those dealing with working-class life (hitherto absent from school novels). But these books usually portrayed women in a very biased manner. Frith describes the discomfort of her own female pupils when confronted with images of women restricted to 'good', (devoted mothers with no life of

73

their own) or 'bad', (going to pubs, having boyfriends, neglecting the children). 'Kes' and 'Zigger Zagger' are particularly guilty of this type of portrayal. The few novels by women on the syllabuses are preoccupied with sex, boyfriends, pregnancy, and social life. The higher up the age range, the harder it is to find novels which allow an active role to female characters. The assumption that boys are reluctant readers follows them from primary to secondary school, leading to teachers choosing books specifically aimed at keeping their attention. Boys may be able to identify with such books, but Frith argues that the models of women in them are frequently negative and distorted ones. It could be argued that the existence of such books in the school curriculum is legitimate since they accurately reflect 'real life'. In reality, men are more likely than women to be breadwinners; women do occupy a narrower range of jobs than men. In reply it must be pointed out that many men do not conform to the stereotypes of males in books. Most men are not heroes or strong protectors of weak females. Many men are unemployed, unable to be breadwinners. 'Real life' is in fact far more varied than the books show.

Staffing in schools

Sixty per cent of teachers in all types of school are women, but they are not evenly distributed among all levels of teaching. School staffing is extremely hierarchical, with the greatest number at the lowest level, that of the Scale 1 classroom teacher. In 1976, 61.6 per cent of headships were held by men (DES statistics). In secondary education the position of women is even weaker, as Table 2 demonstrates.

What the pupils perceive from this is that men are in charge. Most subjects have a male head of department, the exceptions being obviously 'female' subjects such as office arts and home economics. A woman deputy head (the only position where women are equal with men) frequently has responsibility for 'girls' welfare', pastoral care, and social

Table 2 Percentage of teachers on each scale, by sex, 1983

	male %	female %
head	84.3	15.7
deputy head	62.7	37.2
senior	80.9	19.0
scale 4	77.9	22.1
scale 3	62.9	37.0
scale 2	49.8	50.1
scale 1	37.4	62.5

Source: DES Statistics of Education 1983.

events, and is often jokingly referred to as the 'nits and knickers deputy'. Male deputies can be found in charge of discipline, curriculum development, and external examinations, all of which carry a higher status than personal welfare.

The relative position of men and women in school staffing provides a close approximation to the roles of men and women in the wider society. Teaching is often regarded as a female occupation because it is concerned with caring and the welfare of the young. Jobs such as nursing and social work are also predominantly female, but in both of these, as well as in teaching, it is men who achieve the top positions and consequently the top salaries; in yet another way, pupils are learning a lesson about gender roles in society. The most damaging message of gender role streotypes, according to Sharpe (1976) is that they foster the belief that girls should not be as clever as boys. 'If you want to attract boys, don't start showing how clever you are' a teenage girl is quoted as saying in Sharpe's study, with long-term implications for subject choice and career aspirations.

Careers, work, and YTS

Conceptions of work are present throughout the school

curriculum. A government report noted:

> 'Boys were more likely to be considering careers involving
> science ... and therefore the career implications of
> omitting from their choices one or more science subjects
> were more evident to them than to girls.'   (DES 1975)

Gender conditioning in schools has serious implications for
career choice. Firstly, the idea is reinforced that certain types
of knowledge and skills are more appropriate for one sex than
the other, at school and at work. Secondly, through the
learning process, pupils develop not only skills in subjects but
a self-concept, a view about the self. If the self-concept is
based on a stereotyped and distorted picture of male and
female roles, vocational choice will reflect this. The qualifications pupils leave school with can affect the careers that are
open to them, so the option choices made two years before
leaving are going to have an impact on possible careers. If
girls are being channelled away from sciences and technical
subjects, they are in fact being denied the same career
opportunities as boys.

Another aspect of the predominance of girls in domestic
subjects is that it suggests that only they need these skills,
since their future is to have a home and children. Sharpe
(1976) found that most of the girls in her survey were very
much influenced by ideas of gender stereotypes, and would
consider only a narrow range of occupations, with implications
for the level of pay they would earn.

Owing to the poor employment prospects of most young
people today, many are now entering a year of training when
leaving school – the YTS scheme. The school leaver statistics
prepared by local Careers Offices provide a picture of the
destinations of girls and boys. In 1984, in Skelmersdale New
Town, a town with a school leaver unemployment rate of 39
per cent, more than three times as many school leavers
entered schemes than found work. A stereotypical picture
emerges when the placements of girls and boys on Mode B
schemes are examined (Mode B schemes are special workshops

set up for training purposes, while Mode A schemes involve training on employers' premises):

Table 3   YTS placements in Skelmersdale, 1984

Skill	no. of boys	no. of girls
building	17	0
catering	7	9
clerical	5	20
community care	0	19
computers	11	7
engineering	38	0
gardening	6	0
graphics	6	0
hairdressing	0	10
metalwork	7	1
motor vehicle	23	0
painting	5	1
retail	7	19
sewing	0	10
upholstery	6	0
woodwork	13	0

Source: Careers Service, Lancashire County Council, School Leaver Destinations 1984.

The picture which emerges from these figures is even more traditional than may be found in school option groups and the world of work generally. One of the Mode B workshops in Skelmersdale had attempted to break down prejudices held by boys and girls towards particular trades. Some success was achieved, but the workshop experienced outside pressures from critics objecting to their 'interference' with the stated interests of school leavers.

There is increasing evidence to suggest that YTS placing is flying in the face of the principles of equal opportunity (see p. 16), undoing some of the work that has been going on in schools to widen the horizons of pupils. With no immediate prospect of more job opportunities for young people, and with the extension of the YTS scheme to two years, sociologists will increasingly be turning their attention to the impact of YTS on the aspirations of school leavers. The advent of YTS has effectively raised the school leaving age, particularly since social security benefits are reduced if a person refuses to go on a scheme. It is appropriate, therefore, to include the YTS programme as part of the education system of Britain. The indications at present point to a return of selection, this time at post-sixteen instead of eleven, and the undermining of the opportunities for girls that have been developing in schools.

Activities

Observation of early socialization

A lot of information can be gained by just looking at human behaviour. Before the observation starts, make a list of examples of behaviour you might expect to see. During the observation, use a notebook to record what you see according to the categories on your list. Also note down examples of unexpected behaviour.

1 Arrange to visit a pre-school play-group to observe the different play patterns of girls and boys. Observe which toys and equipment girls and boys are using and how each sex plays with them. Are girls or boys noisier? Do girls or boys get reprimanded for noisy behaviour?
2 Spend some time with young children of different ages in your neighbourhood; ask them what presents they received for their previous birthday or Christmas; ask them what they would like to be when they grow up. Write down your observations.
3 Investigate the subject matter of comics for girls and boys. What type of subjects feature most in the comics designed for each? Make lists of the topics found in each. How are male and female portrayed in the comics?

4 Examine the boys' and girls' toys in a toy shop. Pay particular attention to the packaging: what sort of pictures and colours are used? Which sex is depicted on the packaging? Are the shelves labelled 'boys' toys' and 'Girls' toys'?

Gender differentiation in schools

5 Carry out a participant observation study of each class you attend. To do this you will need the co-operation of a sympathetic teacher. Note down the subject, numbers of male and female students, sex of teacher; count up the number of times males and females are addressed by the teacher, which sex talks the most in discussion; if relevant, which sex is the more disruptive. Note: this activity may be difficult. Teachers can be sensitive if they are aware that their performance is being assessed. If teachers agree to the observation, they may alter their normal behaviour knowing they are being observed. If you decide to proceed unknown to the teacher, think carefully about the ethics of covert observation.

6 Investigate the staffing of your school or college. Who appears to be in charge of the different departments? Which subjects have the most male or female teachers? You may need the co-operation of a member of staff to find out some of this information, especially in a large college.

7 Try to obtain the GCE and/or CSE entries for previous years in your school or college. Compare the male and female entries. In which subjects are boys concentrated and in which are girls concentrated? Have there been any significant shifts in subjects taken by male and female over time?

Note: for nos. 6 and 7 there may be problems in obtaining the information described. As in no. 5, the help of teachers is desirable.

8 Examine the organizational practices in your school or college. Are males and females divided up separately for

any purpose? (e.g. queueing, sport, crafts, seating in classrooms, or examination halls). Is inter-sex competition encouraged? If there is a uniform, how do the rules differ for male and female?

9 Examine the table of examination entries on p. 73. Comment on the following things: the type of subjects in which males or females are in the majority; the type of jobs related to each subject. Find out some information about a selection of 'male' jobs and 'female' jobs. Which have the better pay and promotion prospects?

Further reading

Adams, C. and Laurikietis, R. (1980) The Gender Trap. 1: Education and Work. *London: Virago.*

Deem, R. (1978) Women and Schooling. *London: Routledge & Kegan Paul.*

McRobbie, A. and McCabe, T. (eds) (1981) Feminism for Girls: An Adventure Story. *London: Routledge & Kegan Paul.*

Oakley, A. (1975) Sex, Gender and Society. *London: Temple Smith.*

Sharpe, S. (1976) Just Like a Girl. *Harmondsworth: Penguin.*

Spender, D. (1982) Invisible Women: The Schooling Scandal. *London: Writers and Readers.*

Whylde, J. (ed.) (1983) Sexism in the Secondary School Curriculum. *London: Harper & Row.*

Whyte, J. (1983) Beyond the Wendy House: Sex Role Stereotyping in Primary Schools. *London: Longman (for the Schools Council).*

4

Education and race

The major explanations for educational inequality may also be applied to issues of race. This chapter examines in detail the processes by which the children of ethnic minority groups appear to be disadvantaged in the education system.

As a background, it is necessary to look at the history of race relations and the origins of racism in Britain.

Racism in Britain

Discrimination against people on grounds of their racial origin has been well documented. Research carried out in the mid-1960s by Daniel (1968) demonstrated widespread discrimination against ethnic minorities, but above all black people, in housing, employment, and commercial services. In this research, actors belonging to different ethnic groups were used to apply for jobs, rented accommodation, and a range of services. The research resulted in the strengthening of race relations legislation. Smith (1977), in a repeat of Daniel's study, produced similar findings, and a recent survey found that 35 per cent of people admitted to feeling racial prejudice. All ethnic minority groups who reside in Britain experience some degree of discrimination and racism but it is black people who bear the brunt of it. Many nationalities and races have come to Britain as immigrants, but for many people, 'immigration' means black immigration.

In some parts of Britain, such as East London and Liverpool, black people have suffered arson attacks on their homes and physical attacks on themselves and their children. A Home Office Report in 1981 stated that Asians were 50 times and West Indians 36 times more likely to be attacked in the street than white people (HMSO 1981), but only a tiny proportion of complaints about racial discrimination ever reach the courts. A wealth of data is available showing that black people suffer the worst housing, employment, wages, and living conditions in Britain. In education, the children of some ethnic minority groups, particularly West Indians, appear to fare badly in terms of acquisition of qualifications and entering further and higher education.

The origins of racism

Surveys into racial attitudes reveal how deeply ingrained racism can be among white people. White racism involves a notion of the superiority of white people. Racism has been the official ideology of nations, the most notable being Nazi Germany, where millions of people were killed because of their race. Racism is institutionalized, so that procedures set up by public organizations automatically discriminate against certain ethnic groups. One example is the existence of a language test for jobs where the language of the worker is irrelevant to that job. Racism is also present in the media – on the news, in documentaries, and in comedy programmes, members of ethnic minorities are frequently shown in a strereotyped or unfavourable light.

Racism in the UK can be traced back to Britain's historical relations with black people. British 'imperialism' – the growth of the British Empire – involved the conquest of countries with black populations so that their natural resources – required for the expansion of British industry – could be exploited. The black inhabitants of these countries, which were 'underdeveloped' by British industrial standards, were portrayed as primitive, savage, and heathen in the media of the day, and in children's books – one famous example being the 'Little Black Sambo' series. Most white people's perception of black people were entirely formed through these media. The tiny minority who actually went to Britain's colonies went to rule over the black people. Their only relationship with them was as master and servant. British people benefited economically from this relationship because of the flow of cheap resources to Britain. Even today, the British enjoy many products because, as a result of its historical relationship with Third World countries, Britain can exploit those countries for their resources and labour.

Immigration in Britain

There were relatively few black people living in Britain before the Second World War, although it was by no means an ethnically homogeneous nation. As described above, most white people's knowledge of black people came through the stereotypes in the media and literature. After the War there was a severe labour shortage in British industry. The public transport system and the newly-established National Health Service also needed large quantities of labour. A solution was sought in Britain's colonies and former colonies. The National-ity Act of 1948 granted British citizenship to the inhabitants of countries in East Africa, Asia, and the West Indies, actively encouraging them to settle in Britain. London Transport set up a recruiting office in Trinidad, textile firms sent representa-tives to India and Pakistan, and the Minister of Health went in person to the Caribbean to find staff for Britain's new

83

hospitals. As a result of this policy, Britain's black population grew from half a million in the late 1940s to 1.85 million by 1971, 3.4 per cent of the total population.

The government believed that a free flow of labour would reduce wage costs and aid the expansion of the economy. Little concern was shown as to how the immigrants would fit into British society. Most of the immigrants occupied the most unpleasant and badly paid jobs and found only poor housing conditions to live in, which reinforced prejudices and stereotypes. The official approach was to underplay cultural differences and encourage 'assimilation', as exemplified by Collins (1957), who wrote that blacks should 'not contrive to observe folkways alien to British society'. The ingrained racism of white British people was severely underestimated. It had not been anticipated that immigrants would be subjected to widespread discrimination and attacks. Incidents of racist behaviour which did occur were considered as evidence of failure on the part of blacks to assimilate.

Racial discrimination in Britain

The government was shaken out of its complacent attitude towards race relations by the riots which took place in the summer of 1958, most notably in Nottingham and in Notting Hill in London. These riots were sparked off by white attacks on black people. Quite clearly, failure to assimilate could not be blamed on this occasion, but racism was not yet accepted as a widespread phenomenon. The judge in a court case arising out of the riots blamed a 'handful of young white hooligans'. Nor until 1965 was racial discrimination made illegal.

By the 1960s the economy was experiencing the start of the recession with all the accompanying social problems, such as housing shortage and unemployment. Much media coverage was given to speeches blaming immigration for Britain's problems. The most publicized views were those of Enoch Powell MP, who advocated the repatriation of black immigrants, even suggesting that they be given financial assistance to return to their countries of origin. He argued that failure to do so would lead to bloodshed on Britain's streets. Coverage of Powell's views was often accompanied by sensationalist descriptions of black harassment of white people, none of which were ever proved. Despite this, and also despite the fact that, in every year but one since the War, emigration has exceeded immigration, Parliamentary measures to limit immigration were popular among those people who felt most threatened by the recession. London dockers even staged a protest march in support of Powell's views.

Governments have viewed racial conflict as a numbers problem, rather than as a consequence of white racist attitudes. Both Labour and Conservative Governments passed successive Immigration Acts, restricting immigration so severely that it is now extremely difficult for black people to settle in Britain. At the same time, white attacks on black people continue and increase. Some local councils are confronting the problems by measures such as evicting known white, racist families from council property, but in the main the law seems ineffective in dealing with white racism.

Research into the black experience in Britain has followed three distinct trends. The earliest research concentrated on the degree to which black people had assimilated into the British way of life. This emphasis was superceded by studies of ethnic culture, much of it commissioned by the Institute for Race Relations, now called the Commission for Racial Equality. More recently the purpose of research has been to describe the black experience in terms of disadvantage and discrimination. The most significant research is concerned with education. Explanations for working-class failure at school did not satisfactorily explain the problems faced by black children. In 1971 Coard pointed to the disturbing evidence of a significant over-representation of West Indian children in schools for the educationally sub-normal (ESN schools). Since then, a variety of explanations for black educational performance have been put forward.

The educational performance of black children

Education is seen as the major factor affecting the future of black children because of the link between schooling and occupation. There has, however, been little recent systematic research into the performance of ethnic minority children in British schools. The Department of Education and Science (DES) stopped collecting information on the performance of 'immigrant' children in 1972.

A survey of Local Education Authorities in the late 1960s found that black children tended to occupy the lowest streams in secondary schools and few gained grammar school places (Townsend 1971). The findings of Coard (1971) were confirmed by DES statistics: 0.68 per cent of non-immigrant children attended ESN schools, but for West Indians the figure was 2.33 per cent.

Since the surveys referred to here, research has been localized and small-scale. Between 1966 and 1975, the Inner London Education Authority (ILEA), with large concentrations of ethnic minority children in its schools, tested 4,269 immigrant and 22,023 non-immigrant pupils in English, mathematics, and verbal reasoning. The findings replicated the results of earlier studies. West Indian children had the poorest performance among immigrant children, followed by Asians. West Indian children wholly educated in Britain did better than those only partially educated here. No evidence was found that the gap in performance was closing over time.

The National Child Development Study, a longitudinal survey of all the children born in one week in March 1958, when assessing the children at the age of sixteen in reading and mathematics, found that first-generation immigrants (including West Indians, Asians, Irish, and Europeans) had lower scores on both tests than the indigenous population. For second generation immigrants, only the West Indian sixteen year olds had significantly lower scores.

Performance in public examinations shows the same pattern. The findings of a survey of school leavers in six local authorities for 1978 and 1979 are shown in Table 4.

Table 4 Academic performance, by ethnic group, 1981

	West Indian %	Asian %	all leavers %
English O Level/ CSE Grade 1	9	21	29
maths O Level/ CSE Grade 1	5	20	19
5 O Levels/ CSE Grade 1	3	18	16
1 or more A Levels	2	13	12
went to university	1	3	3

Source: Rampton Report 1981.

These findings come from the Rampton Report of 1981, and seem to indicate that the problem of underachievement lies with children of West Indian origin. Asian children seem to be performing on an equal level with the indigenous population. The report explained underachievement as a result of poor pre-school facilities for West Indian children, and inappropriate school curriculum and teacher attitudes. Reeves and Chevannes (1981) have criticized this approach, arguing that underachievement is mainly a result of the disadvantaged class position of West Indian families. West Indians are far more likely than Asians to have working-class backgrounds.

Other aspects of the black school experience have been documented more recently. Wilson (1983) shows that a disproportionate number of black pupils are suspended from school. Stone (1981) argues that the stereotypes that teachers possess about black pupils actually divert them away from academic courses towards 'ethnic' pursuits such as steel bands and athletics. Evidence of such stereotypes may be seen in a submission to the Rampton Commission reported in the *Times Educational Supplement*: 'If there is a difficulty of cultural identity among second generation West Indians, there is also much to counterbalance that deficiency including their natural sense of rhythm, colour and athletic prowess' (cited in Carrington 1983). Encouraged by the media attention given to the performance of black sports men and women 'sport may provide the school with a convenient and legitimate sidetrack for its disillusioned black low achievers' (Carrington 1983). Carrington argues that sport is used in schools as a mechanism for social control of black pupils – it compensates for academic failure and contains pupil rebellion. Troyna (1979) suggests that black pupils may connive in this process by using sport to gain social acceptability or to 'colonize' one area of school activity. They may see sport as a viable route to success, but will be doomed to even greater disillusion since, in reality, no more than a tiny proportion succeed in the sporting world.

In 1985 the Swann Committee reported its findings. This committee had continued the research of the Rampton Commission into the educational performance of ethnic minority children, in the wake of the social disturbances in Brixton, Toxteth, and Moss Side. Swann's findings did not greatly differ from the Rampton Report. It largely confirmed earlier studies: of the ethnic minority groups, West Indian children seemed to do worst in school, although Swann reported a slight improvement over the 1981 averages; Asian children were performing on a similar level with white children. The Report points out that the figures in their research are only averages, and conceal wide variations in performance. The main explanation given for underachievement is the relative economic disadvantage of black families in Britain. However, it is suggested that this explanation is not entirely satisfactory since it does not explain the performance of Asian children. Asian families are on average worse off than white families but there is no significant difference between the educational performance of the children. The Report cautiously suggests that differences in lifestyle and the tightly-knit family structures of Asian homes may be the key factor, but admits that there is insufficient evidence to support this theory.

The Swann Report argues that there can be no single explanation for unequal educational performance, and that it is misleading to seek for one. It demonstrates the strong and indisputable evidence of racism and prejudice which black pupils suffer in British schools, marking a departure from earlier approaches to the problem which denied that widespread racism existed. The Report makes a range of recommendations but it is too soon as yet to comment on their implementation.

Explanations for the educational performance of ethnic minority children

Race and intelligence

As outlined in Chapter 2, there is strong support in the educational world for arguments both in favour of and against the idea that intelligence is inherited. Before the Second World War, almost all differences in educational performance were explained by inheritance. When black recruits to the American armed forces obtained lower average scores in intelligence tests, it was attributed to their race. Since the War, genetic arguments have become less accepted. It has been pointed out that the average performance of black soldiers in tests at the start of the Second World War were an improvement on their scores in the First World War. This improvement has been attributed to the bettering of living conditions for black people in the USA over that period of time. A difference was also noted between the scores of soldiers from the Northern and Southern states of America. Again, living standards tended to be higher for Northern black people than for those in the South.

Acceptability of the idea that race and intelligence were related was renewed by American psychologist Arthur Jensen in a widely-publicized article in 1969. Jensen argued that it was impossible to explain performance differences between white and black people by reference to environmental factors. The persistence of the 15-point difference in scores suggested very strongly that black people were indeed genetically less intelligent than white people.

Jensen's arguments were based on the research which had been carried out with twins reared in different environments. Doubts about the validity of the twin research have been used to criticize the work of Jensen. (See p. 25). It could be argued that estimates of the inheritence of intelligence are based on tests given to particular populations, and it is not possible to generalize from them to other populations. There is also disagreement between supporters of the genetic theory about the proportion of intelligence which can be explained by heredity. Pilkington (1984) argues that even if there were significant genetic differences between black and white people, that does not discount the possibility of boosting intelligence by environmental factors. Jensen himself attributes some of the gap in educational achievement to environment factors.

Pilkington (1984) speculates as to why the genetic arguments were resurrected in the late 1960s. He suggests that Jensen's theory came at a convenient time for the American government. Economic growth was slowing down, which made it difficult to keep up educational expansion. With inequalities between black and white still persisting despite the relative affluence of the post-War period, the genetic theory of intelligence could be used to justify reductions in educational expenditure – valuable resources should not be used to change the unchangeable.

The influence of the family

Critics of the hereditary theories of intelligence often cite differences between the home backgrounds of black and white children as an explanation for differential performance. Rex (1982) suggests that the traumatic history of the West Indian people, including slavery and forcible migrant labour, destroyed their culture and family system, with far-reaching implications for the West Indian family in Britain. In the West Indies themselves, a number of different family forms exist, particularly prevalent being the 'matrifocal' family, headed by the mother who may or may not be married. Economic and emotional support for the family is provided by the mother and her female relatives. Pilkington (1984) suggests that the less clearly defined kinship relations of the West Indian family may cause the children to possess a less secure sense of identity.

Taylor (1981) suggests that although West Indian parents regard education highly, 'they seem to lack understanding of the developmental importance of play, toys, communication and parent-child interaction in the early years'. Also, because West Indian parents are reputed to be far stricter than average white parents, it could be argued that the West Indian child is less well prepared for school than a white child.

The National Child Development Study (1980) points to the economic disadvantage of West Indian homes in explaining educational differences. In housing, employment, and wages, West Indians seemed to fare the worst of all immigrant groups with school-age children. Economic factors may also explain why West Indian children are likely to be cared for by child minders in their early years. There has been a higher proportion of one-parent families among West Indians, and also the traditionally low pay of male West Indians tends to force mothers out to work. Research has shown that the quality of care given by child minders is very varied, and that the very poor black families may resort to cheaper, unregistered – and therefore uninspected – child minders.

The better educational performance of Asian children has been attributed to family structure. The different history of Asian culture has enabled the family to remain relatively stable, and to retain its language, religion, and traditions. Settlement in Britain has not eroded this stability. While the image of the non-English-speaking Asian mother staying in the home, and the arrangement of marriages for daughters may be a stereotype, Asian families in Britain do seem to live in more tightly knit communities than West Indian families and, as evidenced by the existence of many Asian community associations, they appear to possess a strong sense of ethnic identity, which the dominant white culture has, it is claimed, destroyed among West Indians. A discussion of the family life of ethnic minority groups needs to acknowledge the danger of stereotyping. Much of the research referred to has a tendency to treat the white British family as the norm.

In the USA Katz (1968) points out that the emphasis on the disadvantaged upbringing and language of black children ignored the fact that being black meant a double handicap (Deutsch, Katz, and Jensen 1968). The white environment, particularly in America, was threatening and stressful, placing a drain on a black person's educational performance. Low expectations of success further affected performance.

The role of the education system and teacher attitudes

Traditionally, explanations for educational performance concentrated on what pupils brought to school: on their culture and home background. More recently, an alternative approach has been to look at the role the school plays in perpetuating inequality. It is argued that schools are permeated by white, middle-class values, reflected in the curriculum, teaching methods, and forms of assessment. Schools are 'ethnocentric' – they reflect the culture of one group in society. They are biased against the culture of ethnic minority groups. Pupils from these groups 'fail' according to the standards set up by a white-dominated education system.

Not only is the curriculum ethnocentric, but the black experience is almost totally excluded, or appears in a very limited and stereotyped way. Straker-Welds (1984) brings together a series of articles examining different aspects of the school curriculum and multi-cultural initiatives. Gill (1984) demonstrates the racism inherent in geography syllabuses. Black people are generally portrayed as primitive, living in straw dwellings, or as providing valuable resources for 'us'. Their poverty is explained by reference to their large families, such as in this example from a GYSL Resource Sheet (Geography for the Young School Leaver) on Calcutta:

'It is well known that millions have the pavement as their

92

home. Streets are strewn with sleeping families at night. But the pavements remain almost as littered during the day. It is evident that thousands of people either lack the energy or the need, because unemployed or unemployable, to move from their gutterside homes.'   Gill (1984:4)

File and Hinds (1984) discuss the issue of history, quoting a young black woman who had been told that black people had no history. They argue that in most schools, history is élitist, sexist, racist, and Eurocentric. Lessons about the 'discovery' of America and other countries ignore the rich culture of the indigenous inhabitants and suggest that 'the white man' was the universal benefactor of these peoples. Only in the topic of slavery do black people appear, and they are depicted in textbooks packed like sardines in ships or being punished for disobeying their 'masters'. The many examples of slave rebellion, even of the successful Haiti revolution, are ignored, as are examples of black achievements. Everyone has heard of Florence Nightingale, but few know about the equally notable black nurses, such as Mary Seacole, who went to the Crimea.

To consider other areas of the school curriculum: in literature, black writers are absent from syllabuses and school libraries; the music studied is Western; cookery is English, and in languages, bi-lingualism is regarded as a hindrance and not an asset. Ethnic minority children are rarely given the opportunity to take public examinations in their own language, and other cultures are excluded from the syllabuses of most subjects in most examination boards, as Mukhopadhyay (1984) shows. Straker-Welds's book shows that even mathematics and science are not neutral, in their use of illustrative material, and ignore the scientific and mathematical developments of the Chinese and the Arabs.

The Rampton Committee (1981) recommended an overhaul of the school curriculum, mentioning in particular library resources and the employment of multi-ethnic education advisers. Tibbetts (1984), accounting for black underachievement in schools, argues that children feel accepted and wanted when their cultural origins are acknowledged.

Of particular concern to some teachers has been the growth in incidents of racist attacks in and outside schools, orchestrated by Fascist political groups. This issue has even been dealt with, in a mild form, in the popular children's television series Grange Hill.

Giles (1977) examined teacher attitudes, finding that over two thirds saw West Indian pupils as being less able and more of a discipline problem than white pupils. He demonstrated a large-scale stereotyping of black pupils and low expectations of their performance by teachers. Troyna (1978) outlines the 'self-fulfilling prophecy' created by such teacher attitudes: black pupils encounter teacher prejudice and low expectations, leading them to become rebellious, thus reinforcing the negative stereotypes. A higher proportion of black pupils get suspended from school than of white pupils.

Teachers appear to be reluctant to confront issues of race, perhaps fearing to unleash latent racism in their white pupils. When a college lecturer encouraged white police cadets to write about their attitudes towards race, and publicized the extremely racist results of that exercise, he feared dismissal from his job. The attitudes he revealed appear to be widely held by many people working with the public and give some indication as to why black pupils 'fail' in British schools.

The effect of self-esteem

There is evidence which suggests that West Indian children enter school with a negative image of themselves. Milner (1975) explored the attitudes of children of different ethnic groups towards their own and other races. Children in the sample were asked to choose between two dolls, of which one represented the child's own racial group. One hundred per cent of white children and 76 per cent of Asian children chose the doll of their own race, but only 52 per cent of West Indian children did so. When asked 'Which doll would you like to be?', 82 per cent of the West Indian children chose the white doll. Bagley and Coard (1975) also found this in a small scale study of West Indian children in two London schools. Such findings might explain why West Indian children underachieve in school. They appear to have internalized a negative self-image which could encourage them to 'give up' in school.

Similar research to that of Milner carried out more recently presents less clear-cut findings (e.g. Davie and Norburn 1980, Louden 1978). These studies suggest that children from minority ethnic groups are less likely to reject images of their own race, particularly older children. Bagley, Mallick, and Verma (1979) found that self-esteem among black pupils was lowest when they were in schools with a small concentration of black children. Also, West Indian boys tended to have lower self-esteem than West Indian girls.

Cultural deprivation

Explanations which concentrate on disadvantaged home background and low self-esteem have been widely adopted to account for black underachievement, both in Britain and America. They provided the starting point for the policies of the Head Start Programme in the USA and those arising from the Plowden Report in Britain. These policies were based on the idea that black and working-class children were culturally deprived. Education was seen as a way of compensating for the cultural deficiences in the black or working-class home.

Cultural deprivation theories have come under severe criticism both in Britain and the USA. Firstly, the theory suggests that black culture is inferior. Labov, researching into the language of black children in the USA, concluded that the language spoken by black people was different from that of whites but certainly not inferior. It was a complex language with a logical grammar and vocabulary (see p. 32–3). Black children underachieved in American schools because their language was looked down upon and discouraged. Likewise, in Britain the Creole dialect spoken by many working-class West Indians possesses an English vocabulary with some different grammatical rules influenced by West African languages. Wight and Norris (1970) found no evidence that Creole interfered with the classroom interaction of West Indian children in infant schools. It could arguably be the cultural bias of the teachers of black children which contributed to their educational underachievement.

Carby (1982) argues that it is racist to suggest that black people possess a deficient culture which is to blame for their children's failure in school. Cultural deprivation theory absolves the education system itself of any responsibility. Lawrence (1982) rejects the idea that West Indian culture was destroyed by slavery, pointing to strong evidence for the retention of religion and family forms despite the trauma of slavery to which black and West Indians were subjected.

Educational policies and multi-cultural education

Official acceptance of cultural deprivation theory has contributed to the improvement of conditions in schools in the poorest parts of Britain, where large concentrations of black people tend to be found. Likewise, in the USA, the Head Start Programme did put resources into some ghetto schools and provide educational opportunities for black pupils which would otherwise not have occurred. What the programmes could not do, in Britain or America, was change the basic economic inequalities which underlie the differences between racial groups in both societies.

Compensatory policies have been uneven and inconsistent. Much funding has gone into English As a Second Language (E2L) provision for Asian children, but almost no extra money has been provided to help West Indian children with language difficulties. As Coard showed in 1971, the problems of many West Indian children have been dealt with by putting them into ESN schools. Although the Rampton Report (1981) concluded that language was not a significant factor in the underachievement of West Indian children, some research shows evidence that possession of a dialect can interfere with the development of writing (Wight 1971). Edwards (1976) argues that the language problems of West Indian children have been greatly underestimated, finding that performance in comprehension tests was strongly affected by Creole.

The Bullock Report (1975) called for sympathy for and a positive attitude to the language and culture of ethnic minority children in British schools. In contrast with the assimilationist policies of the 1950s and 1960s, when the idea was to get the immigrants to accept British ways of life as quickly as possible, most schools with a sizeable black population now encourage and celebrate the cultural diversity of their pupils. Particularly in primary schools, in Birmingham, Bradford, or East London it is as common to find the celebration of Divali as of Christmas. Steel bands are as common as orchestras in secondary schools with a large West Indian population, and many schools, such as in the ILEA, have Caribbean studies or Black studies on the syllabus.

Such initiatives are known as multi-cultural education. They are based on the assumption that the curriculum of schools has been partly responsible for the underachievement of black pupils. Multi-cultural education does, however, cover a multitude of different things, from E2L, the provision of Halal meat for Muslim pupils' dinners, to the inclusion of 'ethnic' topics in the curriculum. Some black educational researchers criticize such types of multi-cultural education for failing to confront the provision of a good basic education for black pupils (e.g. Stone 1981). It has been suggested that curricular innovations such as 'black studies' channel black pupils away from acquiring the basic qualifications acceptable to employers and further education institutions. Carby (1982) condemns multi-cultural education as part of a strategy to control black pupils, arguing that an awareness of black history and culture may be used by schools to quell the rebellion of black pupils.

In the USA during the late 1960s educational policies for ethnic minorities involved ensuring that schools had an evenly-balanced racial mix. This meant the movement of pupils by bus each day from black neighbourhoods into schools in white areas. This policy was known as 'bussing', and its success has been disputed. Black spokespersons wanted to know why it was mainly black pupils who were bussed, and there were protests in white areas, organized by racist groups. Kirp (1980) argues that bussing was successful and widely accepted in the USA. Because of the tendency of neighbourhoods to assume an ethnic identity, bussing was seen as the only way to achieve racial integration in schools. In Britain, where policies designed to aid the integration of ethnic minority pupils have concentrated on the curriculum, there has been no national policy in favour of physically transporting pupils to ensure racial balance. Schools generally reflect their neighbourhood, and initiatives have been localized, not generated from the Department of Education and Science.

Alongside multi-cultural education there have been initiatives in schools with the aim of combating white racist attitudes, known as 'anti-racist education'. This is based on the view that the main cause of black people's problems is white racism. Black people are not themselves 'a problem'. White racism is the reason black people occupy the poorest paid jobs, worst housing, and why their children don't do so well in school. Anti-racist education is aimed at white pupils, who sometimes turn the anger and frustration they experience as a result of their bleak employment prospects against the easily-identifiable target of black pupils. Anti-racist education tries to replace the negative and stereotyped perceptions of black people which the white pupils possess. Gill (1984) shows how the subject of geography can be used to confront such perceptions. She uses a 'brainstorming' technique to unearth the stereotypes of 'Africa', such as 'Tarzan', 'tribal dances', and 'starving people', to discuss with pupils how stereotyped images are formed, then gets pupils involved in project work designed to help them discover for themselves the reality of Africa. (Brainstorming is a teaching technique whereby pupils are asked to write down or say anything suggested by a word or an idea.) Anti-racist education also involves careful choice of books and educational materials as well as racism awareness training for teachers.

There has been an attempt to evaluate the effectiveness of multi-cultural education and anti-racist education in Britain. A three-year project was set up, and reported in 1975, called 'Problems and Effects of Teaching about Race Relations', involving a large number of teachers. The teachers adopted one of three teaching strategies in dealing with race in the curriculum: A: playing the role of neutral chairperson in pupil discussions, B: making clear their personal commitment to fighting racism, C: using improvised drama. The teaching about race using these three strategies took place with fourth-year pupils. Findings suggest that method B, in which teaching about race was direct and open, was the most effective in increasing the tolerance of white pupils towards black people.

Activities

Attitudes towards race

1 Devise a questionnaire about racial attitudes. This could be done as a group activity. Use the questionnaire in your school/college. This activity needs careful preparation. Questions to be included need to be discussed to ensure that they do not produce biased answers. The results of your survey could lead to a fruitful class discussion.

Experience of discrimination

2 This activity was carried out in a College of Higher Education for a whole week to highlight conditions in South Africa. It requires the co-operation of teaching and non-teaching staff. Post notices in key parts of the school/college building, such as dinner queues, outside classrooms, in changing rooms. The notices should present messages such as 'No persons wearing T-shirts to queue here', 'Pupils from ..... street will be served meals last', 'Pupils wearing white socks are to change for games first'. This activity will have the greatest effect if

the 'rules' are strictly enforced. As a follow-up, pupils
can be questioned about their experience of discrimination.

3 For this, the whole class or a group within a class will
need to read either of the first two books in the list which
follows these activities. Discuss the experiences of the
main character in the chosen book, around the following
questions: in what ways was she discriminated against?
How did it affect her? What strategy did she adopt for
coping with discrimination? Were all her experiences a
result of her skin colour? What suggestions would you
make to reduce discrimination in Britain?

Racial stereotypes

4 Collect an assortment of magazines, newspapers, and
also use video recordings of programmes which feature
black people. Analyse their content for examples of
racial streotypes. This could include: a 'head count' of
ethnic groups appearing in the media; listing the different
ways in which black people are portrayed; observing
what types of advertisements on television black people
are used in.

5 Analyse the content of school textbooks with the same
purpose as in activity 3. With the co-operation of
teachers, a search through stores of old textbooks,
particularly in the field of geography, may reveal some
spectacular examples of racial stereotypes. Discuss the
extent to which members of ethnic minority groups are
absent in school books and syllabuses.

Multi-cultural society

6 Research your neighbourhood or town. Find out which
groups have settled in the area in the past 100 years. Find
out if the different groups have left examples of their
culture. For example, places of worship, styles of
architecture, language, shops, styles of dress. Find out
what factors caused migration into the area.

Further reading

For descriptions of white attitudes to black people:

Emecheta, B. (1983) Adah's Story. London: Fontana. A vivid, autobiographical account of the experiences of black immigrants to Britain in the early 1960s.

Riley, J. (1985) The Unbelonging. London: The Women's Press. Describes the experiences of a young West Indian girl in a hostile, all-white school in the 1960s, and the culture shock she faces when she returns to Jamaica as a university graduate.

Novels and stories by Doris Lessing set in Southern Africa in the post-War period describe colonial attitudes. Granada Books produce several volumes of her short stories written over a long period of time.

For a slightly different angle on race and immigration:

Hong Kingston, M. (1977) The Woman Warrior. London: Picador. This deals with the experiences of a Chinese family in California.

For basic background information on race in Britain:

Pilkington, A. (1984) Race Relations in Britain. London: University Tutorial Press.

Wilson, M. (1983) Immigration and Race. London: Penguin. This book also gives details of legislation relating to race as well as legal rights.

5

The process of schooling

Introduction

This chapter considers the processes taking place within schools and their contribution in shaping the educational experience, attitudes, and success or failure of pupils. The research which has taken place into the process of schooling adopts a varied, sometimes innovatory, approach. The explanations of pupil performance generated by this research do not easily slot into the main theoretical perspectives outlined elsewhere in this book. Although many of the studies in this chapter are ultimately concerned with the same area – differential educational performance by an identifiable group of pupils – there is a common rejection of the traditional methodology of empirical studies in education.

The sociology of education has changed considerably since the passing of the 1944 Education Act. Much of the early research of this period was designed to evaluate the success of government policies in achieving educational equality. The research focused on the social structure, and the empirical studies produced large quantities of statistics. No attention was paid to the daily life of schools, the behaviour of pupils, or the attitudes of teachers. Sociologists adopted what has been termed the 'black box' approach, concentrating on the school only in terms of its relationship with the outside world. The research was concerned with the outcomes of education, such as the percentage of working-class boys who went to grammar school.

Above all, the research dealt with what was easily quantifiable. Perhaps this was because, as Karabel and Halsey (1979) suggest, the presentation of an impressive array of statistics enhanced scientific credibility in the eyes of politicians, who were frequently the source of finance for the research. Sarup (1978) argues that this research assumed that reality exists unproblematically; the researchers presuppose a passive view of individuals, and see life in terms of 'technical problems'. They deny the significance of the active role played by the participants in the education system, the pupils and teachers. The limitations of this approach have encouraged sociologists in more recent years to investigate alternative ways of analysing education.

Ethnographic studies of education

'Ethnography' is a term borrowed from anthropology. Ethnographic studies involve gaining an intimate understanding of the people being studied, just as anthropologists observe and record the smallest details of everyday life of the group under investigation. Anthropology has taught sociology a lot about methods of investigation and insights into social behaviour.

An important feature of ethnography is that the researcher must be a 'participant observer'. In an educational setting this means either joining the staff of the school as Hargreaves (1967) did, or finding a way of spending as much time as possible with the teachers and/or pupils being studied.

The ethnographic approach rejects the traditional procedures of empirical research such as questionnaires and statistical analysis. The aim is for the researcher to observe with an open mind, and with preconceptions suspended, recording the actual language spoken by the subjects under study. Keddie (1971) used a tape recorder to supplement her own observation and notes. Spender (1982) found that a tape recorder was essential to enable her to quantify the language used by male and female pupils, and she also used video recordings to gain an understanding of non-verbal behaviour which cannot easily be noted down on paper.

The ethnographic approach is useful for studying pupil cultures, and gives insights into the educational experiences of particular groups, such as girls or black pupils. An important feature of the method is that no aspect of human behaviour is considered too insignificant to study, hence the production of some unusual and innovative research.

Classroom studies: the streaming system

During the late 1960s a series of classroom studies was conducted, investigating the effects of internal selection in schools, the streaming system.

Hargreaves (1967) worked as a teacher in a boys' secondary modern school, to carry out a participant observation study of the social effects of streaming. *Social Relations in a Secondary School* has become a classic of this type of research, inspiring many since then. At Hargreaves' school, the boys were divided into four streams from the first year upwards, on the basis of academic ability. This system was very rigid, with very little movement between streams after the first year. Only one boy had ever started in the D stream and ended in the A stream. Hargreaves found that not only was there a close correlation between social class and stream, but that the streaming system produced pupil sub-cultures which led to conflict between pupils. The lower-stream boys had created an anti-school, anti-academic, sub-culture because they had been labelled by the school as failures. These pupils placed a high value on behaviour which teachers would regard as indiscipline. This was in contrast with the top-stream pupils, who accepted the academic norms and values of the school.

Lacey (1970) observed a similar phenomenon in *Hightown Grammar*. This school streamed from the second year onwards. First-year boys were, in the main, committed to the school and well behaved. Streaming destroyed this homogeneity of attitude. Lacey interprets this as a group response to failure. As in Hargreaves' study, lower-stream boys, largely from working-class backgrounds, adopted anti-academic attitudes and behaviour. As a socializing organization, the school was operating as a stratifying device; some pupils were being streamed towards success while others, from working-class backgrounds, were prepared for failure. This significantly affected the jobs the pupils would eventually get.

Studies of teacher attitudes

Keddie, in *Classroom Knowledge* (1971), examined the humanities department of a large, socially mixed, comprehensive school. Her concern was with the knowledge teachers have of pupils and the knowledge the teachers regarded as suitable for classroom presentation. As with the studies of Hargreaves and Lacey, Keddie was interested in the processes involved in the production of academic 'failures'. The classes Keddie studied were unstreamed. Careful observation of teachers both inside and outside the classroom revealed that, although most vigorously denied believing that social class was related to ability, they categorized pupils in the classroom according to social background. The teachers determined this social background, not by intimate knowledge of the pupils, but by superficial characteristics and stereotypes.

Despite the absence of streaming, pupils were still thought of as 'A-streamers' or 'C-streamers', and treated according to these labels. Teachers differentiated between these groups in the materials made available to them. Questions from pupils designated as 'C-streamers' were rarely treated as genuine, being regarded as disruptive or attention-seeking. Questions from 'A-streamers' were evidence of their enthusiasm for learning. Keddie suggests that teachers defined as 'bright' pupils who submitted to their authority without question. She argues that the differentiation of pupils by teachers was as effective as an official streaming system in impeding the progress of working-class pupils.

Keddie's findings have similarities with those of Bowles and Gintis (1976). Also in America, an earlier study by Cicourel and Kitsuse (1963) had examined the academic guidance system in a high school. Guidance staff were known as counsellors. The counsellor's job was to advise pupils about appropriate courses to take at school and future careers. Cicourel and Kitsuse found that the counsellors frequently made stereotyped judgments about the pupils, according to assumed background, class, race, attitudes held, and even the clothes pupils wore. Pupils were 'guided' along directions deemed appropriate by the counsellors. Many pupils effectively had the chance of higher education or particular jobs closed off to them because of the courses they had been steered onto at school.

Most classroom studies are of secondary schools. An exception is Sharp and Green's study of 'Mapledene' infants' school. At this school, the emphasis was on progressive, child-centred education. The curriculum was based on the needs and interests of the child. There were opportunities for children to choose activities and develop at their individual pace. This type of primary schooling has been called 'progressive' and is regarded as a sharp contrast to traditional teaching, where the teacher is an authoritarian figure whose main concern is discipline.

The teachers at 'Mapledene' school were committed to the principles of progressive education but experienced pressures to 'deliver the goods' traditionally expected of schools:

literacy, numeracy, and 'civilizing a deprived portion of the population'. Sharp and Green (1975) found that the effect of progressive teaching methods was remarkably similar to that of the traditional forms of classroom organization that the teachers were opposed to. Sharp and Green concluded that progressive education can actually be used as an effective means of social control. Its therapeutic features make it attractive to teachers and pupils, but in the end the pupils are disciplined to accept authority just as if they had been taught in a more authoritarian manner.

Pupil cultures

Hargreaves and Lacey described how the streaming system of secondary schools led to the creation of an anti-school sub-culture amongst working-class pupils. Willis (1976) turns his attention to the features of that culture in his study of a small group of working-class boys in a comprehensive school. The 'lads', the title adopted by the boys, possessed a culture which reflected working-class culture. A high value was placed on toughness, opposition to authority, and an aggressive attitude towards women. This culture often took the form of boasting in an exaggerated way about sexual experiences, accompanied by graphic physical gestures. The 'lads' used every opportunity to demonstrate their opposition to the values of the school 'in the struggle to win symbolic and physical space' and had become skillful at 'managing' the formal system, to avoid regimentation as much as possible.

Their central aim was the avoidance of work: 'Some of the lads develop the ability of moving about the school at their own will to a remarkable degree. They construct virtually their own day from what is offered by the school' (Willis 1976). Truancy was only one of such tactics. Others included being in the wrong class, finding a quiet corner to sleep, and roaming the corridors during lesson time. The boys were determined to derive as much enjoyment as possible out of school, but not in the way the teachers intended. They claimed that 'having a laff' (Willis's spelling) was their main concern. Willis gives a description of a school outing to a museum. The back seats of the coach transporting them are covered with graffiti and names in indelible ink, and in the museum every possible 'don't touch' sign is blatantly ignored. 'The lads are a plague of locusts feeding off and blackening out pomp and dignity'.

Willis claims that the culture which the boys had created was a contributory factor in preparing them for manual work when they left school. Just as they found enjoyment in the school they saw as oppressive, so they were destined to accept dead-end and boring jobs. Their anti-school culture prepared them for the working-class culture of the factory floor: 'Both share broadly the same determinants: the common impulse is to develop strategies for dealing with blocked opportunities, alienation and lack of control' (Willis 1976). In the final analysis, school has in fact prepared the working-class pupils for a subordinate position in society, and Willis argues that the study exposes the myths about educational opportunities for all.

Willis's study has been criticized for its pessimistic and negative analysis of working-class youth behaviour. David (1985) states that the book reads like a celebration of macho culture in the way Willis appears to admire the 'lads'. The study also implies that the boys' attitudes are the cause of the subordination of women, when in fact the attitudes are a reflection of a society based on male dominance over women. What is also in doubt is Willis's characterization of working-class culture. It seems to be exaggerated and stereotyped. As many teachers (and female pupils) experience, it is normal for male pupils to lay claim to sexual exploits under the impact of peer group pressure, as well as to use grossly colourful language. Willis accepts what the boys tell him at face value, and nowhere in the study is there any evidence that the findings were checked out.

The effect of teacher expectations

Hargreaves (1967, 1972) suggests that because teachers 'know' that, statistically, working-class children do less well at school than do middle-class children, they adopt a fatalistic attitude to those whom they perceive as working-class.

Several small-scale studies demonstrate that teachers are influenced by class stereotypes about pupils. Nash (1973) showed that primary and secondary school teachers in Scotland held strong perceptions about the expected behaviour and performance of their pupils. To investigate this, Nash used a technique known as a repertory grid. Each teacher was presented with three cards with the name of a child in their class on each one. Teachers were asked how each child differed in any significant way from the other two. Teachers used terms like 'noisy', 'bright', 'immature', and 'badly behaved' to describe their pupils. There was a close correlation between the pupils' actual behaviour and the teachers' evaluation of them. Nash concluded that teachers' perceptions of pupils greatly influenced their attainment, and yet there was no significant correlation between the actual and perceived social class of the children. Findings were similar in primary and secondary schools.

Davies and Meighan (1975) examined teacher expectations with regard to gender. Their finding that teachers shared a preference to teaching boys, and the likelihood that this was communicated to the girls goes some way towards explaining why girls' academic performance deteriorates in secondary schools.

Fuchs (1968) describes an innovative approach to discovering the effects of teacher attitudes in New York. She got a group of newly-qualified teachers to tape record their experiences of their first semester (six-month period) of teaching in elementary schools. The teachers start their careers with an open-minded attitude towards their pupils, who came in the main from low income and ethnic minority groups. Very quickly, more experienced teachers inform the new entrants of the 'facts' about their pupils: they come from inferior homes with a low level of culture, as evidenced by the lack of books and newspapers in the homes. One teacher reports being told that the parents care more for partying than the welfare of their children. The implications are that the parents are to blame for the educational problems of the children. The school is absolved of any blame.

At first, the new teachers find it hard to accept this, but by the end of their first six months, are explaining the failure of pupils in the same way as the older teachers. Fuchs explains that the young teachers had been socialized by the attitudes of those around them, and have come to behave towards their pupils in a way which perpetuates their disadvantaged position.

The self-fulfilling prophecy

Closely related to the research into teacher expectations is the concept of the self-fulfilling prophecy. Rosenthal and Jacobson (1968) demonstrate the operation of this phenomenon in their study of the effects of teacher expectations on the performance of elementary school pupils. They measured the intelligence of 20 per cent of the pupils with IQ tests, but assigned scores to them on a completely random basis. This false information was given to the teachers. One year later Rosenthal and Jacobson returned to the school to test the same group for a second time. They found that those who had been assigned high scores in the first test actually achieved high scores in the second test, in some cases significantly higher than their actual first scores. Rosenthal and Jacobson concluded that the children's performance had improved because teachers expected them to. These expectations were transmitted to the pupils by means of facial expressions, postures, touch, and language used, as well as possible changes in teaching techniques: 'Such communications . . . may have helped the child learn by changing his self-concepts, his expectations of his own behaviour and his motivation, as well as his cognitive styles and skills' (Rosenthal and Jacobson 1968).

Rosenthal and Jacobson's research illustrated a classroom phenomenon which had not hitherto been investigated. Their research has been criticized for an imprecise explanation of how teachers' expectations operated on the pupils. Rosenthal and Jacobson did not observe the classroom behaviour of teachers. They could only speculate upon the details of the process. Critics also point out that the IQ tests used were of poor quality, and many of course reject the validity of IQ tests altogether. Finally, other similar studies have been unable to replicate Rosenthal and Jocobson's findings.

The performance of a pupil according to a teacher's expectations has been termed the 'self-fulfilling prophecy'. This means that something happens because it is expected to happen. The operation of the self-fulfilling prophecy can be demonstrated in the commercial world by the way shortages of products have occurred after media announcements that they would occur. Leigh (1977) outlines the five stages of the self-fulfilling prophecy in the classroom:

1 Teacher has expectation of pupil performance.
2 Teacher communicates that expectation to the pupil.
3 Pupil receives that expectation.
4 Pupil develops a change in self-concept which leads to changed behaviour.
5 Change in pupil performance occurs.

Leigh states that this sequence is not inevitable. Pupils may ignore the message received from the teacher or fail to receive it.

Labelling theory

The theory of labelling has been developed from studies of crime and deviance. Becker (1963), with whom the term originated, argued that behaviour in itself could not be deviant; it only acquired that character when it was labelled as deviant. Labels arise when rules are established. A deviant person is someone to whom the label of deviance has been successfully applied. This can be illustrated by examples of behaviour which is only labelled deviant in particular places and at particular times. A man pushing a pram would have been regarded as deviant before the Second World War, but not in 1986; the consumption of alcohol is not considered deviant on a beach in Britain but it would be regarded less tolerantly if it occurred in a Muslim country.

In a school, a multitude of rules and regulations exist. Pupils transgressing them are labelled and treated as deviant. But if rules did not exist, such as in the wearing of uniform, a form of deviant behaviour – to turn up for school in jeans, for instance – would cease to exist. Becker sums this up with: 'Deviance is created by society. Social groups create deviance by making rules whose infraction constitutes deviance' (Becker 1963). Labelling occurs in schools when a pupil is regarded as a deviant, either through committal – actual or assumed – of a deviant act. Labels may be assigned to pupils because of stereotyped perceptions held by teachers. Most of these stereotypes derive from images of social class, ethnic origin, or gender.

Labelling has a social-control effect. Being labelled for a minor transgression of the rules may effectively stop the pupil from repeating that transgression. But labelling can also amplify deviant behaviour. Hargreaves (1976) describes how labelling assigns a new status to a pupil. He/she is no longer treated as 'normal' but as a potential 'problem'. The deviant act committed by the pupil comes to engulf them. The pupil starts to develop a self-concept based on the label, which in turn reinforces the label:

'The teacher is to some degree wary of everything he says and does. All his accounts to explain his untoward behaviour are carefully scrutinised and checked by the teacher, who is much more likely to see them as "excuses", prevarications and even lies than as valid reasons . . . "You

112

have to keep an eye on Smith" says the teacher, and additional restrictions are made on his freedom of movement and autonomy.'   (Hargreaves, 1976)

Labelled pupils are also subjected to exclusion or isolation from others. They may be made to sit alone in class or placed in a 'special unit' (sometimes known colloquially as the 'sin bin') with other 'problem' pupils. Hargreaves suggests that it would be surprising if the pupil treated in this way did not react with hostility and frustration. But when he/she does so, the label is reconfirmed. The only way to get rid of the label is to behave according to a code which is considerably less deviant than that of 'normal' pupils. Even if this pattern of behaviour can be achieved, the labelled pupil may be suspected of insincerity, or of 'trying it on'. It becomes increasingly difficult for the pupil to retain a self-concept without the label, and he/she might also reinterpret his/her past behaviour in terms of the label. Hargreaves refers to his own study of 1967 to demonstrate labelling at work. Only A- and B-stream pupils were ever selected as prefects, and lower-stream pupils were frequently excluded from school outings and holidays in case they would cause 'trouble'.

Meighan (1981) describes the ultimate effect of labelling. The labelled person, suffering from isolation, deliberately seeks out the support of people or groups with similar labels. In this way gangs get formed, although they are more likely to manifest themselves outside than inside schools. Meighan points out that schools with the most rigid rules generally produce the most deviants.

The hidden curriculum

The 'hidden curriculum' is a useful concept in discussing the purpose and effects of education. It can be defined as all the things that are learned in schools, other than what is officially timetabled. The hidden curriculum includes attitudes, values, notions of 'normal' and 'not normal'. Meighan (1981) quotes

113

Head (1974) in describing the hidden curriculum:

> 'The hidden curriculum is taught by school, not by any teacher. However enlightened the staff, however progressive the curriculum ... something is coming across to the pupils which may never be spoken in the English lesson or prayed about in assembly. They are picking up an approach in living, and an attitude in learning'.
>
> (Head (1974) in Meighan 1981)

This is transmitted to pupils in a variety of ways: through the rules, routines, and regulations of the school, through the atmosphere, the buildings, and room lay-outs, and through the hierarchical staffing structure.

The concept is easiest to understand through concrete examples. It could be said that the gender stereotyping of school subjects is a value prevailing in schools. Despite legislation, boys and girls still mainly opt for subjects traditionally appropriate to their gender. Pupils receive from teachers and each other strong messages about values. These messages may take the form of disapproval, teasing, or even humiliation, if a pupil expresses an interest in a subject or career outside the 'normal' gender boundaries. Obstructions may be placed in the pupil's way to act as a discouragement. For example, a girl may be warned that she will get her clothes dirty if she attempts vehicle maintenance, or told that the class is full up. 'It is through the unconscious manipulations of teachers using restricted gender definitions ... (which) might enter the hidden curriculum of the school and affect the student's choice of subject' (Macdonald 1981).

Bowles and Gintis (1976) conceive the hidden curriculum as the means by which the attitudes and values of capitalist society are transmitted to children in schools. The hidden curriculum operates to train children for their future role as workers, and teaches them to defer to authority, accept regimentation, and regard inequality as natural. Bowles and Gintis argue that the attitudes and personalities engendered by schools correspond to those of the capitalist economy. The

114

hidden curriculum is the means by which schools: 'create and reinforce patterns of social class, racial and gender identification among pupils, and allocate them to differential positions in the occupational hierarchy of authority and status in the production process' (Bowles and Gintis 1976). The main message of the hidden curriculum is that only a few will succeed in life at the expense of the many who fail.

Many studies demonstrate this aspect of the process of schooling, even if they do not directly refer to the concept of the hidden curriculum: Hargreaves (1967), Keddie (1971), and the 'deschoolers', whose work will be discussed later in this chapter, are a few.

In attempting to illustrate the hidden curriculum, Meighan (1981) uses the analogy of 'haunting' in the ghostly sense, to explain the way society's values invade the classroom. Teachers feel that when the classroom door closes, everything within the room is within their control and direction. But in reality the teacher is not autonomous. The classroom is haunted by 'ghosts': the ghost of the architect who designed the building, the ghosts of the authors of books used in the classroom, and the ghosts of the creators of language. All 'haunt' the educational experience through the messages they carry.

This analogy is useful in explaining the covert, or concealed forces which operate on a social institution like education. Meighan also proposes an alternative analogy, borrowed from electronics – that of transmission through invisible radio waves. He suggests that such analogies avoid the suggestion of conspiracy which some writers imply operates behind the transmission of values.

The concept of the hidden curriculum has had wide-ranging applications, as a method of interpreting everything from day-to-day events in schools, to the functioning of the education system as a whole. It is a concept which is mainly used by critics of the processes taking place within the education system, but research findings which demonstrate its operation have been used to support widely differing perspectives. Some

115

take a pessimistic view, viewing the hidden curriculum as evidence of the enduring power of capitalist socialization processes. A variant on this suggests that society should be 'deschooled'. By taking education out of state control, a major social institution would be removed from the tentacles of capitalist values.

The hidden curriculum is a useful concept in the sociology of education, particularly in assisting the interpretation of the effects of schooling, but too much emphasis on it may lead to a neglect of the effects of the official curriculum. The hidden and official curricula are not two distinct things. Whichever perspective of education is taken, they both reflect the character of the wider society.

Alternatives to state education

The sociology of education has been almost exclusively concerned with education provided by the state, which is responsible for the education of over 90 per cent of British children. The research which studies of education have yielded since the Second World War has demonstrated repeatedly that a free education system to which all have equal access does not guarantee equality of opportunities, and there are still significant differences in performance between the social classes, between the sexes, and between the members of different ethnic groups.

Some parents, usually wealthy ones, do not believe that a state schooling is capable of providing their children with a good education. They opt out of state education and send their children to fee-paying private schools. Others have doubts about the curriculum of state schools, and may question the ideology which prevails in such schools. There have always been schools which cater for people with distinctive philosophical or political views, and which offer innovative or experimental curricula and school organization. These schools have become known as progressive schools.

The deschoolers

The theory of 'deschooling' offers an analysis of the functions of education in a capitalist society and proposes alternatives. This theory arose from the publication in 1971 of *Deschooling Society* by Ivan Illich, a former Roman Catholic priest. Illich spoke out against the institutionalization of education. He argued that the obligatory nature of schools hindered the learning process. In schools, children were taught, they did not learn. The acquisition of grades and qualifications were a substitute for real learning. Children who achieved low scores in tests learned to accept it as a personal failure, when it was the system that was at fault. Illich argued that the role of education is to indoctrinate children with the values of a capitalist economy. This stifles their instinctive curiosity and imagination. They are forced to conform to rules which they have had no part in devising.

Around the same period of time, a series of critiques of education were published, in general agreement with Illich's views. This has been referred to collectively as a deschooling 'movement'. There was, however, no organizational connection between these writers. Some wrote from a philosophical standpoint, while others wrote as a result of their experiences and observations as serving teachers in the American school system. They share a common belief that education as currently constituted is a significant cause of the problems of modern industrial society, and that these problems could be remedied by educational reforms.

Reimer (1973) takes up the deschooling theme of the relevance of what is taught in schools. He gives examples of real learning through real life experiences. He quotes examples from the work of teachers among illiterate Latin American peasants. The peasants learned to read and write, not through the formal methods of schooling, but through their own motivation, and through teaching related to the needs and interests of their daily lives.

Goodman (1973), in a discussion of the nature of education,

argues that school is a mere auxiliary to the educational process. Schools make children believe that life is inevitably routine, depersonalized, and graded. He asks: what evidence is there to suggest that basic skills like reading and writing would not be picked up in the course of natural experience? Words should be learned as the need arose, in real-life situations, not as mere symbols. Holt (1969) shows graphically that the methods of teaching simple school subjects seem almost deliberately designed to confuse children. He argues for a radical rethink of teaching methods, but points out that the most effective methods are slower, since they are geared to the pace of individual children. Such a slow process would not be tolerated by the existing school system, nor by teachers, who are under pressure to show an impressive array of examination grades in a given time.

The alternative system proposed to the deschoolers throws an interesting light on their understanding of the role of education. Reimer and Illich propose that, since education is a basic right, each person should be guaranteed by law a quota of education for each year of life. This quota could be used as quickly or as slowly as the individual required. There would be equality of educational facilities and no entrance requirements. This would, it is argued, break down class distinctions.

Goodman, pointing out the wastage in schools (estimated at 85 per cent at elementary level), suggests that there could be special academies for the 15 per cent of the school population who were capable of completing the hurdles of state examinations. Illich suggests that any parent who wanted additional educational facilities for the children should be free to purchase it, as long as the basic rights of access to schooling were guaranteed.

Deschooling, in its analysis of the role education plays, is influenced by Marxist ideas, although its ideas for the reform of education are not Marxist. On examination, the deschoolers' educational proposals appear remarkably similar to what already exists. Currently all children have equal access to state, primary, and secondary education, both in Britain and the

118

USA. Parents can choose to pay for alternative services. In both countries a private sector exists to cater for those who reject state education. It is a valid criticism that schools do not enjoy equality of facilities, but the deschoolers' proposals make no mention of methods of financing education to achieve this. More seriously, it could be argued that a society in which freedom of choice is available only to those with sufficient wealth cannot have an egalitarian system of education. The freedom to purchase a privileged education is one way in which social inequality is perpetuated.

The deschooling critique makes many valid points about the curriculum on offer in state schools, and the preoccupation with grading and examinations. These are bound to place limitations on the learning process and teaching methods. They place both teachers and pupils under great pressure. In France and Japan – countries where examinations are extremely important as a passport to higher education and future employment – the high rate of teenage suicides is thought to be related to examination stress.

The deschoolers all emphasize that education should be relevant to real life. They assert that schooling would not need to be compulsory if the curriculum was attractive to children. An interesting point is that when children themselves are asked to describe their ideal schools, their proposals are often very similar to those of the deschoolers, as Blishen (1971) discovered.

The School That I'd Like (Blishen 1971) is a collection of secondary-age pupils' views on education entered for a competition in 1967. Although outside the field of sociology and research, the book is a useful source of data about children's perceptions, not least because of the essential honesty of these children. Many astutely size up the functions of education. 'Children do not want to be taught at, but want to find things out for themselves', writes one, anonymous child. A seventeen year old writes: 'I consider it essential that the school should change with the body of pupils it contains and with the society in which they must be adapted to live'. A thirteen year old must sum up the views of all pupils when she writes: 'I always think it is most important for a subject to be taught interestingly . . . the worst thing in a lesson is boredom'.

The comments of these children express accurately many of the views of deschooling. The problem for sociology is that the deschoolers do not appear to see a connection between the curriculum and teaching methods of schools and the role of education as a whole. It is this which lays deschooling open to the most serious criticisms. The representatives of the idea seem to conceive of an education system operating in isolation from the other institutions of society. They believe that it is possible to change education without major political and economic change. Deschooling seems to gloss over the wealth of evidence which points towards an umbilical link between the structure of society and education systems.

Illich discusses the educational failure of children from low-income families, despite the massive increase in educational expenditure in America in the 1960s, but attributes this to the character of schooling, not to inherent inequalities in the society. Educational research both in the USA and Britain has demonstrated the close connection between educational performance and social class, but Illich does not consider class in his analysis of education.

Illich argues that deschooling could 'destroy the reproductive organ of a consumer society', which ascribes to education a far greater influence than it can possibly possess. Bowles and Gintis (1976) point out the fundamental error of deschooling. Writers like Illich, while offering a useful analysis of the process of schooling, blame social problems on the education system, rather than on the economic system which education serves.

Knowledge and control

'How a society selects, classifies, distributes, transmits and evaluates the educational knowledge it considers to be

120

public reflects both the distribution of power and the principles of social control within that society.'
(Bernstein 1973b)

A previous section has outlined the ways in which the 'hidden curriculum' of a school helps to maintain values, beliefs, and attitudes. But the central feature of schooling is the transmission of knowledge. The knowledge which has been selected as appropriate for transmission to children is known as the curriculum. A typical school curriculum may appear to contain a large and varied selection of subjects and skills, but it will be only a very small part of the knowledge and skills available in society. A school curriculum represents a choice that has been made by persons in charge of the school. This choice may reflect their individual interests or prejudices, as well as the nature of local employment; in Liverpool, a maritime city, navigation is likely to be available as a GCE subject, while forestry is common in schools in North Wales. Above all, the school curriculum reflects the culture, values, and beliefs of those in positions of power over the education system.

Bernstein (1973b) demonstrates that knowledge as transmitted in schools is highly stratified. It is divided into different fields which carry different social evaluations and rewards, as well as leading to a stratified employment structure. He argues that the education system of Europe is based on 'a model of "bookish" learning for medieval priests'. What counts as valued knowledge in schools is based on:

1 Abstractness.
2 An emphasis on written rather than oral literacy.
3 Individualism, as opposed to group activity and assessment.

Bernstein also points out that, below higher education level, the ways in which teachers are permitted to transmit knowledge are very limited, particularly in England. The curriculum is spelt out and syllabuses are explicit. There is a

121

very strong separation between theory and practical knowledge. Subjects containing a lot of 'theory' have a higher status than 'practical' subjects like woodwork. The assessment and streaming of pupils is based on this separation between subjects. Pupils in lower streams are most likely to be following a curriculum consisting of practical and basic subjects, while those in higher streams concentrate on academic subjects requiring a lot of written work.

As schooling progresses, knowledge becomes increasingly compartmentalized. Subjects are taught in isolation from each other. Teachers are expected to be passionate advocates of their subject, and frequently acquire an identity in terms of that subject. Pupils are encouraged to develop subject loyalty. The integration of subjects is resisted, and when it occurs, limited. At a school in St Helens 'integrated humanities' appeared on the timetable as 'history and geography' because of parental objections.

Pupils are encouraged 'to work as isolated individuals with their arms around their work' (Bernstein 1973b). They are socialized into the idea that knowledge is private property. Helping neighbours with their work may be discouraged, or even punished. The teacher has maximum control of the learning process, effectively policing the pupils. Teaching is also an isolated activity. Most teachers dislike the presence of other adults in their classroom. 'Team teaching' has never been adopted in more than a handful of schools.

As children get older, the teaching they experience becomes increasingly 'teacher-centred' and less 'child-centred'. This is frequently the way teachers prefer. Delamont (1976) refers to the research which monitored the curriculum innovations introduced to cope with ROSLA, (raising of the school leaving age). Of 100 teachers studied who were teaching 'Nuffield science', only a handful practised the learning-by-discovery methods advocated by the designers of the syllabus. This was found to be the case in practice of the Schools Council Curriculum Project. Few teachers relished the 'chair-person' role. In both studies, the majority of teachers observed adapted the new curricular material to the traditional teacher-centred methods.

Knowledge as defined by a school excludes the everyday, 'commonsense' knowledge possessed by pupils, brought with them from their homes. Although only fiction, the example of *Kes*, by Barry Hines, illustrates this well. The pupil is a failure in school terms but possesses a wide knowledge of birds of prey and is a self-taught expert in the art of training kestrels. This impresses his schoolmates and teacher but has no validity in the school curriculum, and will not help him get a job. Language is another area where school values serve to denigrate pupils' own language. Dialect is not considered valid language in school written work. In the past, Welsh children were punished for speaking Welsh at school, while West Indian children who spoke Creole are frequently disadvantaged when being assessed.

Delamont (1976) discusses the extent of control that teachers have over pupils and over the knowledge which is presented to them. In the interests of keeping control, teachers do not welcome pupil interventions during lessons, even when they are related to the subject matter being studied. Delamont argues that the teacher's role involves being able to think quickly when something occurs which is outside his/her 'script'. Unlike many other professionals, teachers get little opportunity to consult with colleagues while working. This means that teachers must always act hastily against anything which may threaten their control.

Pupils quickly learn the extent to which their outside knowledge is acceptable. Teachers may have a quite tolerant attitude towards 'less able' pupils, perhaps making an effort to base lessons on their interests and concerns. At the end of term such pupils may be allowed to bring in pop records. While the pupils may prefer this to lessons solely reflecting the teacher's interests, it can be seen as an effective means of control, and demonstrates that the pupils are regarded as inferior. Keddie (1971) showed how teachers were selective in the knowledge that they gave out to different groups of children, reserving the more intellectual aspects of a subject for pupils they regarded as 'A-streamers'!

Much of what is considered valid knowledge in schools is remote from many pupils' experience. Vulliamy (1978) illustrates this by reference to music. Classical music is the preserve of a minority of people in society at large. Even fewer school pupils are fond of it. On music syllabuses in schools this minority music is the only type considered 'real'. The sort of music most young people favour is dismissed as unworthy of consideration, because it is 'commercial' and, therefore, not 'art'. Music in schools is the music of the past – passive listening rather than active participation is encouraged, and there is no opportunity for pupils to compose their own music. Above all, there is an almost total neglect of American and non-European music. Music in schools is treated as an élite activity. Lessons in individual instruments are not generally free of charge, and the instruments themselves are beyond the pockets of most families. Some local education authorities are even cutting music tuition in schools in order to make financial savings, which will make music even more the preserve of a minority.

The knowledge which is contained in any one subject is organized throughout schooling in a hierarchy. 'The ultimate mystery of the subject is revealed very late in the educational life' (Bernstein 1973) but only to a select few. Most pupils only have access to a very limited amount of knowledge in each subject. This process enables a minority to pose as 'experts' and 'specialists', in which role they can command high rewards, which further perpetuates the status of their subject. The school system is highly competitive. In many schools pupils are ranked, given a class 'position' according to examination results. These results may determine their future course of study. Many schools operate a 'house' system, and organize competitive activities between 'houses'. Knowledge is not regarded as a right but as something which must be won. The examination or grading system exists to encourage this competition, and offers an acceptable explanation to those who 'fail'.

Bernstein argues that the role of the whole system of education is concerned with social control. Every aspect of schooling is part of the controlling process. Control operates at two levels: firstly, and most obviously to pupils, the teacher has control. Teachers control knowledge in classrooms as well as the behaviour of their pupils. Delamont (1976) demonstrates the extent of this control. Teachers have the legal right to comment on, and hence control, the clothing, hairstyles, footwear, language, behaviour, and cultural interests of their pupils. In addition, 'society gives teachers the right of access to what we can call "guilty knowledge" about pupils ... IQ, reading age, other teachers' opinions, confidential medical and family data' (Delamont 1976). Knowledge of confidential details about pupils gives teachers great power, and can affect the way pupils are treated. Some kinds of private knowledge may lead to more lenient treatment of pupils, such as in cases of bereavement or parental divorce. Delamont comments that teachers spend a lot of time thinking and talking about pupils, and that teachers' perceptions of pupils are crucial in classroom interaction and the control process. At the disciplinary level of control, a wide range of sanctions is available, ranging from physical violence to systematic humiliation. Teachers may differ about what sanctions they should practise, such as whether to support the abolition of corporal punishment, but few question their right to use sanctions at all.

The power that teachers have to control their pupils does not exist independently of the control that society as a whole exerts over education. Most teachers do not discipline pupils because it gives them personal satisfaction. Teachers themselves have little autonomy in the classroom. It can be argued that every aspect of the education process exists to perform a wider function, that of establishing control over society's future workforce (see the outline of the conflict perspective, pp. 43–7). The curriculum, hidden curriculum, teaching styles, disciplinary procedures, and staffing structure are all an essential part of the control process, the 'ideological state apparatus' referred to by Althusser (see p. 45).

Johnson (1976), in a discussion of the historical development of state education, suggests that control of the masses was the main concern of those who initiated state education. The best-known forerunners of state schools, such as those established by Joseph Lancaster, all tended to emphasize discipline, submissiveness, and competition between pupils, as well as rigid religious values. It was no accident that the state system, developing from the 1880s, should incorporate these principles, which are still with us today.

Activities

Examine the labelling process

1 All schools and colleges have individuals who have acquired a label of some description. Choose one such person. Observe the ways in which that person is treated and talked to by staff and students. Note down how this differs from the way others are treated.

2 Discuss with the chosen person how they feel about the label they have acquired. Does it affect their behaviour? Try to trace back, with their help, how the label developed.

Note: 1 and 2 touch on sensitive areas. The persons chosen to study may resent being studied in this way. Possible responses may be non-cooperation or deliberate sabotage of your research. Be aware of the pitfalls. If you encounter any, it may offer a valuable experience of research problems!

3 Observe teachers in the classroom. Do they have any noticeable attitudes which are displayed to students? Are different students treated in different ways? Try to analyse why the atmosphere varies from class to class, and the role the teacher plays in this.

Anti-school sub-cultures

4 Identify a group at your school or college that appears noticeably anti-school in its behaviour. List the different ways in which members of this group behave in class and in the institution generally. If a streaming or setting system operates, see what positions the members of the group occupy. How does their behaviour affect them? Are they excluded from activities or privileges?

5 Interview a member of a sub-culture (this could be a persistent truant or someone who is constantly being disciplined) as if their behaviour was a 'career'. Try to find out how they became a . . . (truant, 'troublemaker', etc.) Find out how they see their role developing and what they really feel about school.

The hidden curriculum

6 Find out and note down the behaviour which is rewarded and that which is punished in your school or college. Do the persons who are constantly being rewarded/praised have anything in common? Do the same for those always in trouble.

7 Try to find out from teachers what criteria are used in grading work and assessing students. Ones to look out for are: neatness, punctuality, 'co-operative' attitude, 'does what he's/she's told', 'comes from a nice home'. Sort these words and phrases into categories. Count up how many of them are directly related to academic performance.

Further reading

The aim of this list is to give a taste of the range of studies available.

Blishen, E. (1971) The School That I'd Like. *Harmondsworth: Penguin. Very easy to read and an entertaining view of children's perceptions of education.*

Delamont, S. (1976) Interaction in the Classroom. *London: Methuen. Deals with the many and varied factors which enter teacher/pupil interactions.*

Fuchs, E. (1968) 'How Teachers Learn to Help Children Fail'. In N. Keddie, (ed.) (1978) Tinker, Tailor . . . the Myth of Cultural Deprivation. *Harmondsworth: Penguin. A detailed account of a teacher's first six months in a New York elementary school.*

Hargreaves, D. (1967) Social Relations in a Secondary School. *London: Routledge & Kegan Paul. One of the first 'classroom studies'.*

Hargreaves, D., Hester, S., and Mellor, F. (1975) Deviance in Classrooms. *London: Routledge & Kegan Paul. Harder to read than Hargreaves (1967) but contains useful verbatim accounts of classroom interaction.*

Holt, J. (1969) How Children Fail. *Harmondsworth: Penguin. A criticism of education by one of the 'deschoolers', based on his experience teaching in America.*

Willis, P. (1981) Learning to Labour: How Working Class Kids Get Working Class Jobs. *Aldershot: Gower. Colourful and entertaining verbatim accounts of the anti-school behaviour of a group of boys, which contrasts with the harder-to-read theory section.*

References

Adams, C. and Laurikietis, R. (1980) *The Gender Trap 1: Education and Work*. London: Virago.

Althusser, L. (1969) *For Marx*. London: Allen Lane.

— (1972) Ideology and Ideological State Apparatuses. In B.R. Cosin (ed.) *School and Society: A Sociological Reader*. London: Routledge & Kegan Paul.

Bagley, C. and Coard, B. (1975) Cultural Knowledge and Rejection of Ethnic Identity in West Indian Children in London. In G. Verma and C. Bagley (eds) (1975) *Race, Education and Identity*. London: Macmillan.

Bagley, C. and Verma, G. (1979) *Racial Prejudice: the Individual and Society*. London: Saxon House.

Bagley, C., Mallick, B., and Verma, G. (1979) Pupil Self-Esteem: A Study of Black and White Teenagers in British Schools. In G. Verma and C. Bagley (eds).

Barton, L. and Meighan, R. (eds) (1978) *Sociological Interpretations of Schooling and Classrooms: a Reappraisal*. Driffield: Nafferton.

— and Walker, S. (eds) (1983) *Race, Class and Education*. London: Croom Helm.

Becker, H. (1963) *Outsiders*. Oxford: Free Press.

Bennett, N. (1976) *Teaching Styles and Pupil Progress*. London: Open Books.

Bereiter, C. and Engelmann, S. (1966) *Teaching Disadvantaged Children in the Pre-School*. New York: Prentice-Hall.

Bernstein, B. (1973a) On the Classification and Framing of Educational Knowledge. In R. Brown (ed.) *Knowledge, Education and Cultural Change*. London: Tavistock.

— (1973b) Social Class, Language and Socialisation. In J. Karabel and A.H. Halsey (eds) (1979) *Power and Ideology in Education*. Oxford: OUP.

Blishen, E. (1971) *The School That I'd Like*. Harmondsworth: Penguin.

Bocock, R.(ed.) (1980) *An Introduction to Sociology: A Reader*. London: Fontana.

Bourdieu, P. (1973) Knowledge, Education and cultural change. In R. Brown, (ed.) *Knowledge, Education and Cultural Change*. London: Tavistock.

Bowles, S. (1978) Unequal Education and the Reproduction of the Social Division of Labour. In J. Karabel and A.H. Halsey (eds) (1979) *Power and Ideology in Education*. Oxford: OUP.

— and Gintis, H. (1972) I.Q. in the Class Structure. *Social Policy* 3 (Nov.–Dec.): 65–96.

— (1976) *Schooling in Capitalist America*. New York: Basic Books.

Braverman, H. (1974) *Labor and Monopoly Capital*. New York: Monthly Review Press.

Brown, R. (ed.) (1973) *Knowledge, Education and Cultural Change*. London: Tavistock.

Bullock Report (1975) *A Language for Life*. London: HMSO.

Carby, H. (1982) Schooling in Babylon. In Centre for Contemporary Cultural Studies *The Empire Strikes Back*. London: Hutchinson.

Carrington, B. (1983) Sport as a Side-Track. In L. Barton and S. Walker (eds) *Race, Class and Education*. London: Croom Helm.

Cashmore, E. and Troyna, B. (eds) (1982) *Black Youth in Crisis*. London: Allen & Unwin.

Centre for Contemporary Cultural Studies (CCCS) (1981) *Unpopular Education: Schooling and Social Democracy in England Since 1944*. London: Hutchinson.

— (1982) *The Empire Strikes Back*. London: Hutchinson.

Chicago, J. (1982) *Through the Flower: My Struggle as a Woman Artist*. London: The Women's Press.

Cicourel, A. and Kitsuse, J. (1963) *The Educational Decision Makers*. New York: Bobbs-Merrill Co. Inc.

Clark, B.R. (1962) *Educating the Expert Society*. San Francisco: Chandler.

Clarricoates, K. (1980) The Importance of Being Ernest . . . Emma . . . Tom . . . Jane: The Perception and Categorization of Gender Conformity and Gender Deviation in Primary Schools. In R. Deem (ed.) *Schooling for Women's Work*. London: Routledge & Kegan Paul.

Coard, B. (1971) *How the West Indian Child is Made Educationally Sub-normal in the British School System*. London: New Beacon Books Ltd.

Coleman, J.S. *et al.* (1966) *Equality and Educational Opportunity*. Washington DC: US Government Printing Office.

Collins, R. (1971) Functional and Conflict Theories of Educational Stratification. In J. Karabel and A.H. Halsey (eds) (1979) *Power and Ideology in Education*. Oxford: OUP.

Collins, S. (1957) *Coloured Minorities in Britain*. London: Lutterworth.

Cosin, B.R. (ed.) (1972) *School and Society: A Sociological Reader*. London: Routledge & Kegan Paul.

Cuff, E.C. and Payne, G.C.F. (eds) (1979) *Perspectives in Sociology*. London: Allen & Unwin.

DES (1975) Curricular Differences for Boys and Girls. *Education Survey* 21. London: HMSO.

Dale, R., Esland, G., Ferguson, R., and Macdonald, M. (eds) (1976) *Schooling and Capitalism*. London: Routledge & Kegan Paul.

Daniel, W. (1968) *Racial Discrimination in England*. Harmondsworth: Penguin.

David, M. (1985) Education. In M. Haralambos (ed.) *Developments in Sociology: An Annual Review, Vol. I*. Ormskirk: Causeway Press.

Davie, A. and Norburn, M. (1980) Ethnic Awareness and Ethnic Differentiation Amongst Primary School Children. *New Community* VIII, nos. 1 and 2.

Davies, L. and Meighan, R. (1975) A Review of Schooling and Sex Roles. *Educational Review* 27:3.

Deem, R. (1978) *Women and Schooling*. London: Routledge & Kegan Paul.

— (ed.) (1980) *Schooling for Women's Work*. London: Routledge & Kegan Paul.

Delamont, S. (1976) *Interaction in the Classroom*. London: Methuen.

131

Deutsch, M., Katz, I., and Jensen, A. (eds) (1968) *Social Class, Race and Psychological Development*. New York: Holt, Reinhart & Winston.

Douglas, J.W.B. (1964) *The Home and the School*. London: Panther.

Durkheim, E. (1956) *Education and Society*. Glencoe: Free Press.

Edwards, B. (1976) Effects of Dialect on the Comprehension of West Indian Children. *Educational Research* 18, no. 2.

Eysenck, H.J. *versus* Kamin, L. (1981) *Intelligence: the Battle for the Mind*. London: Pan.

Fawcett Society (1985) *The Class of '84: A Study of Girls on the First Year of the Youth Training Scheme*. London: Fawcett Society.

File, N. and Hinds, D. (1984) World History in Tulse Hill School. In M. Straker-Welds (ed.) *Education for a Multicultural Society*. London: Bell & Hyman.

Floud, J. and Halsey, A.H. (1958) The Sociology of Education. *Current Sociology* 7, no. 3.

Frith, G. (1981) Little Women, Good Wives: Is English Good for Girls. In A. McRobbie and T. McCabe (eds) *Feminism for Girls: An Adventure Story*. London: Routledge & Kegan Paul.

Fuchs, E. (1968) How Teachers Learn to Help Children Fail. In N. Keddie (ed.) (1973).

Giles, R. (1977) *The West Indian Experience in British Schools*. London: Heinemann.

Gill, D. (1984) Geographical Education for a Multicultural Society. In M. Straker-Welds (ed.) *Education for a Multicultural Society*. London: Bell and Hyman.

Glass, D.V. (1954) *Social Mobility in Britain*. London: Routledge & Kegan Paul.

Goodman, P. (1973) *Compulsory Miseducation*. Harmondsworth: Penguin.

Gouldner, A. (1971) *The Coming Crisis of Western Sociology*. London: Heinemann.

Gray, J.A. (1981) A Biological Basis for Sex Differences in Science? In A. Kelly (ed.) *The Missing Half: Girls and Science Education*. Manchester: Manchester University Press.

Halsey, A.H. (1972) EPA Experiment a Success. *Times Educational Supplement* 6 Oct.

Halsey, A.H., Floud, J., and Anderson, C. (1961) *Education, Economy and Society*. New York: The Free Press.

Halsey, A.H., Floud, J., and Martin, F.M. (1956) *Social Class and Educational Opportunity*. London: Heinemann.

Halsey, A.H., Heath, A., and Ridge, J. (1980) *Origins and Destinations*. Oxford: Clarendon Press.

Hammersley, M. and Woods, P. (eds) (1976) *The Process of Schooling*. London: Routledge & Kegan Paul.

Haralambos, M. (ed.) (1985) *Developments in Sociology: An Annual Review Vol. 1*. Ormskirk: Causeway Press.

Hargreaves, A. (1980) Review Symposium. *British Journal of the Sociology of Education* 1 (2) 211–16.

Hargreaves, D. (1967) *Social Relations in a Secondary School*. London: Routledge & Kegan Paul.

— (1972) *Interpersonal Relations and Education*. London: Routledge & Kegan Paul.

— (1976) Reactions to Labelling. In M. Hammersley and P. Woods (eds) *The Process of Schooling*. London: Routledge & Kegan Paul.

— (1982) *The Challenge of the Comprehensive School*. London: Routledge & Kegan Paul.

Heath, A. (1981) *Social Mobility*. London: Fontana.

Herrnstein, R. (1973) *I.Q. in the Meritocracy*. London: Allen Lane.

Holt, J. (1969) *How Children Fail*. Harmondsworth: Penguin.

Home Affairs Committee (1981) *Racial Disadvantage 1980–1981*. Commission for Racial Equality 1981–82. London: HMSO.

Illich, I. (1971) *De-Schooling Society*. Harmondsworth: Penguin.

Jackson, B. and Marsden, D. (1962) *Education and the Working Class*. Harmondsworth: Penguin.

Jencks, C. *et al*. (1972) *Equality: A Reassessment of the Effect of the Family and Schooling in America*. New York: Basic Books.

Jensen, A. (1969) How Much Can We Boost I.Q. and Scholastic Achievement? *Harvard Educational Review* 39, no. 1.

Johnson, R. (1976) Notes on the Schooling of the English Working Class 1780–1850. In R. Dale, G. Esland, and M. Macdonald *Schooling and Capitalism*. London: Routledge & Kegan Paul.

Karabel, J. and Halsey, A.H. (eds) (1979) *Power and Ideology in Education*. Oxford: OUP.

Keddie, N. (1971) Classroom Knowledge. In M.F.D. Young (ed.) *Knowledge and Control*. London: Collier–Macmillan.

— (ed.) (1973) *Tinker, Tailor . . . The Myth of Cultural Deprivation*. Harmondsworth: Penguin.

133

Kelly, A. (ed.) (1981) *The Missing Half: Girls and Science Education*. Manchester: Manchester University Press.

Kirp, D. (1980) *Doing Good by Doing Little*. Berkeley: University of California Press.

Labov, W. (1969) The Logic of Non-standard English. In N. Keddie (ed.) (1973) *Tinker, Tailor ... The Myth of Cultural Deprivation*. Harmondsworth: Penguin.

Lacey, C. (1970) *Hightown Grammar*. Manchester: Manchester University Press.

Lane, D. (1978) *Politics and Society in the USSR*. London: Weidenfeld & Nicolson.

Lawrence, E. (1972) In the Abundance of Water the Fool is Thirsty: Sociology and Black 'Pathology'. In Centre for Contemporary Cultural Studies (1982) *The Empire Strikes Back*. London: Hutchinson.

Leigh, P.M. (1977) Great Expectations: A Consideration of the Self-fulfilling Prophecy in the Context of Educability. *Educational Review* 29, no. 4.

Louden, D. (1978) Self-esteem and Locus of Control in Minority Group Adolescents. *Ethnic and Racial Studies* 1, no. 2 (April 1982).

Macdonald, M. (1976) Schooling and the Reproduction of Class and Gender Relations. In R. Dale, G. Esland, R. Ferguson, and M. Macdonald (eds) (1976).

McRobbie, A. and McCabe, T. (eds) (1981) *Feminism for Girls: An Adventure Story*. London: Routledge & Kegan Paul.

Meighan, R. (1981) *A Sociology of Educating*. London: Holt, Reinhart & Winston.

Midwinter, E. (1972) *Priority Education: An Account of the Liverpool Project*. Harmondsworth: Penguin.

Millman, V. (1984) The Implications of the New Vocationalism for Girls. *Social Science Teacher* 13, no. 2 (Spring).

Milner, D. (1975) *Children and Race*. Harmondsworth: Penguin.

Mukhopadhyay, A. (1984) *Assessment in a Multi-Cultural Society*. York: Longman for the Schools Council.

Nash, R. (1973) *Classroom Observed*. London: Routledge & Kegan Paul.

National Child Development Study (1980) in Frogelman, K.R. (ed.) *Britain's Sixteen-Year-Olds*. London: National Children's Bureau.

Newsom Report (1963) *Half our Future*. London: HMSO.

Nicholson, J. (1984) *Men and Women: How Different are They?*

134

Oxford: OUP.

Oakley, A. (1975) *Sex, Gender and Society*. London: Temple Smith.

Piaget, J. (1932) *The Moral Judgement of the Child*. London: Routledge & Kegan Paul.

Pilkington, A. (1984) *Race Relations in Britain*. Slough: University Tutorial Press.

Plowden Report (1967) *Children and Their Primary Schools*. London: HMSO.

Rampton Report (1981) *West Indian Children in our Schools*. London: HMSO.

Reeves, F. and Chevannes, M. (1981) The Underachievement of Rampton. *Multiracial Education* 10:1.

Reimer, E. (1973) *School is Dead: An Essay on Alternatives in Education*. Harmondsworth: Penguin.

Rex, J. (1982) West Indian and Asian Youth. In E. Cashmore and B. Troyna (eds) *Black Youth in Crisis*. London: Allen & Unwin.

Richardson, K. and Spears, D. (eds) (1973) *Race, Culture and Intelligence*. Harmondsworth: Penguin.

Rosenthal, R. and Jacobson, L. (1968) *Pygmalion in the Classroom*. New York: Holt, Reinhart and Winston.

Rutter, M., Maughan, B., Mortimore, P., and Ouston, J. (1979) *15,000 Hours: Secondary Schools and Their Effects on Children*. London: Open Books.

Sarup, M. (1978) *Marxism and Education*. London: Routledge & Kegan Paul.

Sexton, P. (1970) *The Feminised Male*. New York: Random House.

Sharp, R. and Green, A. (1975) *Education and Social Control*. London: Routledge & Kegan Paul.

Sharpe, S. (1976) *Just Like a Girl: How Girls Learn to be Women*. Harmondsworth: Penguin.

Skeels, H.M. (1966) Adult Status of Children With Contrasting Early Life Experiences. *Monographs of the Society for Research in Child Development* 31.

Smith, D. (1977) *Racial Disadvantage in Britain*. Harmondsworth: Penguin.

Spender, D. (1980) *Man Made Language*. London: Writers & Readers.

— (1983) *Invisible Women: The Schooling Scandal*. London: Writers & Readers.

Stone, M. (1981) *The Education of the Black Child in Britain*. London: Fontana.

Straker-Welds, M. (ed.) (1984) *Education for a Multicultural Society*. London: Bell & Hyman.

Swann Report (1985) *Education for all: Report of the Committee into the Education of Ethnic Minority Children*. London: HMSO.

Taylor, M. (1981) *Caught Between*. London: NFER/Nelson.

Thornbury, R. (1978) *The Changing Urban School*. London: Methuen.

Tibbetts, C. (1984) Working with the Under-Fives. In Straker-Welds, M. (ed.) *Education for a Multicultural Society*. London: Bell & Hyman.

Townsend, H. (1971) *Immigrant Pupils in England: the LEA Response*. London: NFER Nelson.

Troyna, B. (1978) Race and Streaming: a Case Study. *Educational Review* 30, no. 1.

— (1979) Differential Commitment to Ethnic Identity by Black Youths in Britain. *New Community* VII, no. 3.

Vulliamy, G. (1978) Culture Clash and School Music: a Sociological Analysis. In L. Barton and R. Meighan (eds) *Sociological Interpretations of Schooling and Classrooms: A Reappraisal*. Driffield: Nafferton.

Whylde, J. (ed.) (1983) *Sexism in the Secondary School Curriculum*. London: Harper & Row.

Whyte, J. (1983) *Beyond the Wendy House: Sex-Role Stereotyping in Primary Schools*. York: Longman for the Schools Council.

Wight, J. (1971) Dialect in School. *Educational Review* 24, no. 1.

— and Norris, R. (1970) *Teaching English to West Indian Children*. Schools Council Working Paper 29. London: Methuen.

Willis, P. (1976) The Class Significance of School Counter-culture. In M. Hammersley and P. Woods (eds) (1976) *The Process of Schooling*. London: Routledge & Kegan Paul.

— (1981) *Learning to Labour: How Working Class Kids Get Working Class Jobs*. Aldershot: Gower.

Wilson, M. (1983) *Immigration and Race*. Harmondsworth: Penguin.

Wrong, D. (1980) The Oversocialised Conception of Man in Modern Sociology. In R. Bocock (ed.) (1980).

Young, M. (1961) *The Rise of the Meritocracy*. Harmondsworth: Penguin.

Young, M.F.D. (ed.) (1971) *Knowledge and Control*. London: Collier—Macmillan.

Index

Althusser, L. 45, 51, 126
anti-racist education 98–9

Bagley, C. and Coard, B. 94–5
Bagley, C., Mallick, B., and
    Verma, G. 95
Becker, H. 111–12
Bennett, N. 15
Bereiter, C. 33
Bernstein, B. 31–2, 121, 122,
    124–25
Binet, A. 23
black box 18, 103
Blishen, E. 115
Bourdieu, P. 29–30
Bowles, S. 44
Bowles, S. and Gintis, H. 24, 42,
    45, 50–1, 106, 114–15, 120,
    137
Braverman, H. 40
Bullock Report 97
Burt, C. 4, 23, 25–6
bussing 97–8

Carby, H. 96, 97
careers education 76
Carrington, B. 88

CCCS 17
Chicago, J. 72
child-centred education 17, 106,
    122
Cicourel, A. and Kitsuse, J. 19,
    41, 106
Circular 10/65 10
Clark, B. R. 40
Clarricoates, K. 67
Coard, B. 85, 86, 96
Coleman Report 34–5, 36
Collins, R. 46–7
Collins, S. 84
compensatory education 35, 95
codes 31–2
conflict theory 37, 43–51
consensus 38
Crowther Report 9–10
cultural capital 29–30
cultural deprivation 33–7, 95

Daniel, W. 81
Davie, A. and Norburn, M. 95
David, M. 108
Davies, L. and Meighan, R. 109
Deem, R. 70
Delamont, S. 122, 123, 125

137

de-schooling 116, 117–18, 120
Douglas, J. W. B. 18, 28–9, 34
Durkheim, E. 38

Edwards, B. 96–7
Engelmann, S. 33
English as a second language 96, 97
EPAs 17–18, 29, 34, 36–7
ethnographic studies 103–04
Eysenck, H. J. 26, 58

File, N. and Hinds, D. 92
Floud, J. and Halsey, A. H. 9
Frith, G. 73–4
Fuchs, E. 109–10
functionalism 37–41

GCSE 12, 14–15, 22
gender: ability 65–6, 69; biological differences 62–3; curriculum 67, 72; examination entry 73; reading 66, 74; role models 64–5; socialization 63–5; staffing in schools 74–5; teacher attitudes 68–9, 70–1
Giles, R. 94
Gill, D. 92, 98
Gillie, O. 25
Glass, D. V. 5–6, 54
Goodman, P. 117, 118
Gouldner, A. 49
Gray, J. A. 66

Halsey, A. H. 34, 42–3
Halsey, A. H., Floud, J., and Anderson, C. 9
Halsey, A. H., Floud, J., and Martin, F. M. 8, 17, 27
Halsey, A. H., Heath, A., and Ridge, J. 13, 30, 54
Hargreaves, A. 57
Hargreaves, D. 19, 52, 103,

104–05, 109, 112–13, 115
Heath, A. 55
Head Start 18, 35, 37, 95, 96
Herrnstein, R. 41
hidden curriculum 113–16, 121
Holt, J. 118
Home Office Report 1981 82

Illich, I. 117, 118, 120
immigration 83–4, 85
intelligence 22–6; race 25, 89–90
interactionism 51–3
IQ tests 23–5, 45, 69

Jackson, B. and Marsden, D. 8, 27–8
Jencks, C. 35–6
Jensen, A. 25, 26, 89–90
Johnson, R. 126

Kamin, L. 25–6
Karabel, J. and Halsey, A. H. 48, 103
Katz, I. 92
Keddie, N. 19, 35, 52, 104, 105, 115, 123
'Kes' 74, 123
Kirp, D. 98
knowledge and control 120–26

labelling 111–13
Labov, W. 32–3, 52, 95
Lacey, C. 52, 105
Ladybird reading scheme 66–7
Lane, D. 50
language 31–3, 95–6
Lawrence, E. 96
Leigh, P. 111
Louden, D. 95

Macdonald, M. 114
Marxism 43–6, 47–51

McRobbie, A. and McCabe, T. 67
Meighan, R. 113, 115
meritocracy 41–3
Midwinter, E. 29, 37
Millman, V. 16
Milner, D. 94
MSC 14, 15–17
Mukhopadhyay, A. 93
multi-cultural education 97

Nash, R. 109
Newsom Report 29, 66
Nicholson, J. 65
Norwood Committee 3, 4, 5, 7

Oakley, A. 63, 64

Parsons, T. 40, 41
participant observation 18, 103
Piaget, J. 63
Pilkington, A. 90, 91
Plowden Report 29, 34, 36–7, 94
positivism 51–2
public schools 12–14
pupil culture 104

race: curriculum 92–3;
    discrimination 84–5;
    intelligence 25, 88–90;
    stereotypes 87–8; teacher
    attitudes 94
racism 81–3, 98
Rampton Report 87, 88, 93, 96
raising of school leaving age 5, 10, 78, 122
Reeves, F. and Chevannes, M. 87
Reimer, E. 17, 118
Rex, J. 90
Rosenthal, F. and Jacobson, L. 110–11
Rutter, M. 56–7

Sarup, M. 53, 103
self-fulfilling prophesy 69, 94, 110–11
Sex Discrimination Act 62, 71
Sexton, P. 69
Sharp, R. and Green, A. 106–07
Sharpe, S. 75, 76
Skeels, H. M. 24
Spender, D. 19, 67, 70, 104
Smith, D. 82
social mobility 53–5
Soviet Union 39, 40, 49–50
Stenhouse, L. 122
Stone, M. 87, 97
Straker-Welds, M. 92
streaming 104–05, 106
Swann Report 88

Taylor, M. 91
teacher expectations 109–10, 111
Thornbury, R. 36
Tibbetts, C. 93
Townsend, H. 86
tripartite system 6, 7, 8
Troyna, B. 88, 94
TVEI 16

vocational education 16
Vulliamy, G. 124

Weber, M. 46–7
Whylde, J. 72
Whyte, J. 67, 68, 69
Wight, J. 96
Wight, J. and Norris, R. 96
Willis, P. 52, 53, 107–08
Wilson, M. 87
Wrong, D. 50

Young, M. 3, 42
YTS 15, 16, 76–8